D1155733

Becoming an Online Business Manager

·········· Playing a ··········
Bigger Game with Your Clients
(and Yourself)

TINA FORSYTH

ONLINE BUSINESS MANAGER

Published by:.................A+ Productions
Box 29016
2515 Highlands Rd W
Lethbridge, AB T1J 4Y2
1-888-988-7465
www.PremiumProductServices.com

Author Contact:............Tina Forsyth
(403) 830-4339
tina@onlinebusinessmanager.com

Printed in the United States of America
ISBN: 978-0-9810664-0-0
First Printing September 2008

Editor: Linda Dessau, www.lindadessau.com
Book Cover and Layout Design: Sarah Van Male, www.cyanotype.ca

• Contents •

• FOREWORD

. . . .

Dear Online Business Manager
(and business owner too),

I have hired and fired more than my fair share of Virtual Assistants. Sometimes, it was my fault they didn't work out, but nine times out of ten it was because they didn't have the tools to be worth the investment. They didn't have the skills that are taught in this book. They didn't have the resources that are detailed in this book. And, they didn't have the knowledge that can be gleaned from this book.

As a Virtual Assistant or Online Business Manager, what

do you do for the business owners who hire you? Sure, you make their life easier, but there's so much more you could be doing. You have the power to help them make more money while reducing their costs.

Most VAs and other online support professionals come from an administrative background and have a preconceived notion that their role is to take on the things that the business owner either a) doesn't like doing or b) doesn't know how to do. Their focus is on freeing up the business owner to have more time and a better lifestyle.

But if you want to earn an invaluable place in your client's business, not to mention higher and higher fees, that's not enough.

The key is to change your mindset from how can I make this business owner's life easier to **how can I help grow this business?**

For some, this requires a subtle shift in thinking. For others, the shift is revolutionary. Either way, its impact can speak volumes. And I can tell you that as a business owner, this kind of support is extremely hard to find. I talk to business owners every day who are not getting the kind of support that they need, and it almost always comes down to mindset — their VAs are thinking *administratively* instead of *strategically*. They are great people with excellent skills but their focus rests too narrowly on details and not enough on the big picture.

Having finally learned the secret to healthy, prosperous and meaningful relationships with my team, I no longer hire someone who can simply "help me out." I will only hire people and teams who understand my business and are truly invested in the success and growth of what we are creating. I need to be able to see the ROI from my team members, to measure what they have to offer for my investment. And they need to be able to tell me specifically how they will do this. If they can't demonstrate their value to my business (not just to me) I won't work with them.

Why would they do this — invest so heavily in my success? Because my success is their success. As I make more money, they make more money. As I learn more, they learn more. As I do bigger and bigger things, they do bigger and bigger things. And the reverse is also true. As they learn more, I learn more. As they do bigger and bigger things, I do bigger and bigger things.

As business owners and online support professionals, together we can do more than we can do alone, but only if you make the shift from Virtual Assistant to Online Business Manager.

This book will show you how to make that shift. You'll learn the actual "how to" specifics of the Online Business Man-

BECOMING AN ONLINE BUSINESS MANAGER

ager role and you'll also learn about the crucial mindset that you'll need; because ultimately it's the way you think that will determine your future.

Face it – there is virtually no room for growth or promotion as a VA. You may be able to slightly increase your rates, year-by-year, but that will only get you so far. The OBM, on the other hand, has exponential room for growth — even if you start small you can work to add more value to the business (e.g., managing, planning or leading) and grow into more senior positions over time. This also gives you the opportunity to tie your compensation into the revenues and/or profits of the business which can blow the roof off of what you can make from an hourly wage. The more you help grow your client's business the more you earn as well — everyone wins!

A quick shout out to my fellow small business owners: Why should you read this book? It will give you a priceless and essential understanding of what an OBM can do for you. After all, what's the point of owning your own business? I believe it's to live a better, more fulfilling and financially independent life. And an OBM can help you achieve that. This book will give you insight into how to find, hire and manage your OBM, what expectations to set for them and how to get the best work out of them. If you want to do big things in the world, plan on hiring an OBM and keep on reading to discover how.

And finally, why is Tina Forsyth the one to write this book? Simply put, she is the best of class. She was serving as an OBM before anyone had ever heard of such a thing. She knows more about how to grow an online business than most online business owners. And, most importantly, she has the utmost integrity. She does what she says she's going to do, and then some.

I hope that your professional path is filled with abundance, meaning and joy and that your dreams are realized through an expression of your faith, inner-strength and confidence.

Think big,

Michael Port

Author of *Book Yourself Solid,*
Beyond Booked Solid &
The Contrarian Effect

• INTRODUCTION

I remember graduating from college with my business degree in 1994, and talking with my classmates about our careers. What we wanted to do for a living, our big dreams and goals.

I never could have imagined then what I was really going to be doing when I "grew up": working from home as an online-based business professional. Heck, the Internet barely even existed in 1994 – I don't think I even had my first email address until a couple years later.

It is an awesome world that we live in, where people and

business can be connected beyond the "brick and mortar" of the traditional working environment. I've worked online since 1999, first as an "online community manager" with a start-up magazine for twenty-somethings (boy, were we ahead of our time there - think social networking before there was a term for it) and now as an Online Business Manager for multiple virtually-based small businesses in a variety of industries.

And if one thing is constant in this type of work, it is the fact that there is a HUGE demand for virtual business support, whether the business itself is based online or it's a regular offline business just looking for someone to manage their online presence. The demand is growing so quickly that when my business partner Andrea Lee and I are approached by business owners who are eager to hire online professionals, we are having a hard time finding the help they need.

In particular, we are seeing more business owners who are ready to hire at the management level. They already have teams of virtual assistants, webmasters, designers and other contractors, but what they really need is someone to manage all of this; to *play a bigger role* in their business so that they can grow to the next level. We affectionately coined the term Online Business Manager (OBM) back in 2003, for the simple fact that it seemed to describe best what we do for our clients.

I believe that there are many professionals out there who have the skills to be working as an OBM; they just haven't realized that this opportunity exists. Having worked virtually for almost a decade now, it's easy for me to forget that this way of working is still quite new to most people. And because of that there is a gap between the business owners who are looking to hire OBMs and the people who could potentially be working for them in his role.

Why is there such an alarming gap?

For business owners, it is a matter of not knowing who or what they are really looking for. They may have a faint idea they could benefit from hiring someone to help them manage and grow their business online, but they often have no clue what that role looks like. They aren't clear themselves on what it is they need, which of course makes it quite hard to find someone! Quite often, when we describe the role of an OBM to the business owners we speak to, we hear, "Yes! THAT's exactly who I need on my team ... now where do I find someone?"

And that leads us to the other side of the gap, that there just aren't a lot of people out there who are actively working as OBMs, consciously or unconsciously. So when these clients start looking to fill that role, they are having a tough time finding the person they need.

That's why I'm writing this book ...

I want to close that gap.

Many people – whether they are actively working online or not – have the aptitude and skill set to be able to play this bigger role with clients, they just don't know that the opportunity is out there. Is this starting to sound a little like you, perhaps? Whether you're a new graduate from business school, an experienced former corporate manager, or just someone with the gumption to try it, I hope you're ready to look into a world of immense possibility that's – at the moment at least – still incredibly untapped and woefully under-served. It's kinda like me planning my career back in '94. I had no clue that the option to work this way with clients was even a possibility. Not so many years later, here I am, doing what was once considered impossible.

My mission in writing this book is simple – it's to help you, the future Online Business Manager, open your eyes to the possibility of doing this for a living. And yes, it can be a very lucrative living.

As you read this book, if you find yourself saying, "YES! This is me, I totally want to do this and now I know how – bring it on!" then I will have achieved what I set out to do here. To allow you a space to recognize and hopefully start to move towards playing this bigger role with new and existing clients. Online-based businesses are hungry for this level of support. So let's feed them, shall we?

① TO BE OR NOT TO BE –

....

HOW DO I KNOW IF I'M A POTENTIAL OBM?

"I always wanted to be somebody, but now I realize I should have been more specific."
• L I L Y   T O M L I N

Becoming an OBM is a great choice for anyone who wants professional challenge, stimulating and enjoyable clients and a freedom-based lifestyle. If your spidey senses are already telling you that you're an OBM, feel free to jump ahead to the next chapter. Otherwise, read through this chapter and be sure to spend a few minutes to take the Online Business Manager Aptitude and Attitude Assessment at the end.

There are three types of professionals I believe are especially suited. This isn't an exclusive list by any means – anyone with a marketing mindset and an interest in online business can certainly work towards becoming an OBM. However I consider these folks to be 'on the cusp' of playing this bigger role. What they do already is so close to the role of an OBM, that a simple shift in what they offer could very quickly have them playing a bigger game.

1. Virtual Assistants at the bursting point in their businesses

Virtual Assistants (VAs), those unseen angels who do a variety of tasks for their clients from a home-based office, are struggling; not so much from a lack of business as from an over-abundance of business.

Yes, just like in any professions, there are new VAs out there who are just getting started and are struggling to find clients and get their business off the ground. However many VAs are reaching a critical point in their businesses - having **too much** business coming their way - which in itself brings a whole new set of challenges.

As the founder of an online recruitment and matching service for VAs, I've worked with many hundreds of VAs over the years and have seen a common journey in the growth of their businesses:

- VA starts a new business
- VA gets a few clients and some good experience under their belt
- VA's clients refer them to other potential clients (of which there are always plenty!)
- VA says yes to these new clients and soon has a full business
- VA's business becomes "uncomfortably full. They are getting so much work from various clients that it is hard to keep up (and life all of a sudden is super stressful)

This is what I call the **bursting point**. If you're a VA who's even remotely capable, and you haven't experienced the bursting point yet, trust me, you will. Any VA who has the hot skills that clients are looking for will very soon be full-to-bursting with clients.

It's like eating a huge meal at Thanksgiving; you are so full you could burst, but the food is so good you just can't say no!

The bursting point is your rite of passage

The bursting point isn't necessarily a bad thing, right? You have what you wanted from your VA business, which was to be busy and make some good money. I actually consider the bursting point to be a rite of passage in a Virtual Assistant's business; we all have to go through it in order to define what we do best and who we want to work with.

The thing is, though, that living in the bursting point is not sustainable in the long run. The bursting point is like a bubble, and if you stay in it too long, it is almost a guarantee that you will see the effects of imbalance in your life and that bubble will eventually pop with a messy splat, negative side effects touching everyone within range.

Signs that you are at the bursting point:

- You don't have enough hours in the day to get your work done, and you are falling behind on many of your commitments
- You are feeling overwhelmed and are starting to dread hearing from your clients
- Clients are starting to get upset with you as the work is coming late, is not complete or is incorrect
- Your family and friends are asking you, "Why do you work so much?" or "Are you on that computer again?"
- You don't have time to say yes to any new and exciting projects or clients that come your way (including those that pay a higher rate)
- Work has become a drag; you aren't enjoying it anymore and may even start to avoid it or get depressed (this is a big sign of burnout!)

Does any of this sound familiar to you? If yes, you may very well be at the bursting point in your business.

The cure for some is as simple as saying, "No more clients, I'm full," or even cutting back on your current client load to get back to a more sane and stable pace.

But what if you want to continue to grow your business? What if you are really busy but you're still not making the kind of money you want to make? Or what if you would like to work less but still continue to make a good wage?

You may be ready to graduate to working as an Online Business Manager for your clients.

2. An Online Business Manager in disguise...

There are many online professionals who are already doing OBM level work for their clients but don't realize it, and because of that are selling themselves short in the marketplace and even in the eyes of their current clients.

OBMs in disguise usually come to realize that they are doing more than what the virtual assistant or online support role calls for. It's like the administrative assistant who's really acting as HR Manager. Or the Executive Assistant who's slowly taken on duties of the former Vice President, Operations, only hasn't received the title or pay raise. High time to make an adjustment, wouldn't you say?

There comes a point when they realize that they are "doing more." In some instances, in fact, it's their client who points this out:

My good friend and business partner Cindy Green-way, Author of Virtually Successful, *had this revelation when talking to a client. One day her client said to her "Cindy, do you realize that you are doing much more than any of my previous VAs had done for me?" Cindy hadn't even considered this until her client pointed it out to her, and at first she was confused and asked her client to clarify.*

"Well Cindy, when you're putting together my newsletter, you will actually go ahead and write content to fill any gaps. Any other VA I've worked with in the past has sat back and waited for me to create all the content. It's been a real bonus to have your help there. Also, there was our teleseminar series last month. After you and I had a phone call to discuss the event, you went ahead and started calling and booking speakers, setting up the systems and doing everything needed to run this event. I didn't even have to ask you to do anything, I just knew that you were on task and would take care of it."

Until her client pointed it out to her, Cindy didn't realize she was doing anything out of the ordinary, she was just doing what came naturally to her.

about this in the next section), which is an essential piece of being a successful OBM.

With a strong business background and marketing mindset, anyone can learn the online tools and skills necessary to become an OBM.

After all, business is business. Whether it is an online or traditional business it all boils down to the same thing - create value that people will pay for.

This type of potential OBM is probably one of the most exciting to me, especially when I consider someone like the stay-at-home mom or dad. They have chosen to stay home with their children instead of going back to work, and may have amazing business and marketing skills that are lying dormant for the time being.

Many of them would love to be able to work, if only there was an opportunity that allowed them the flexibility to be home with their children while making a living. I know there are potential OBMs at home watching (yet another!) episode of Barney and wishing they could use their brain for more than memorizing the songs from kid shows.

Or, as anyone who has ever worked in the corporate world knows, there are MANY talented people out there who are under-utilized and essentially miserable in their jobs. (This could be you!) My friend Pamela Slim has an excellent blog called **EscapeFromCubicleNation.com,** where she helps people transform from corporate prisoner to thriving entrepreneur. One of the most common challenges her readers face is that they know they want to get out of their jobs, but they have no idea what to do next.

It is to these business-savvy professionals in particular that I send a "virtual poke" to consider becoming an Online Business Manager.

Online Business Manager Aptitude and Attitude Assessment

Score yourself on a scale of 1-5 for each of the statements below, with 1 being, "No way, that's not me at all!" and 5 being, "Oh, yeah, it's like looking in a mirror!"

I have a general understanding and love of "all things business."	1	2	3	4	5
I thrive on the challenge of being thrown into new (and sometimes uncertain) situations.	1	2	3	4	5
I can easily learn "on the fly" and am not afraid to figure things out as I go.	1	2	3	4	5
I am familiar with and/or have hands-on experience in all facets of Internet marketing.	1	2	3	4	5
I embrace responsibility and am accountable to my commitments.	1	2	3	4	5
I enjoy and understand the value of working with a team.	1	2	3	4	5
I don't mind rolling my sleeves up and getting my hands dirty "doing the work" when required.	1	2	3	4	5
I stay calm in the middle of confusion and chaos, and will naturally take charge to fix a situation when conflict arises.	1	2	3	4	5

I don't take things personally, and know that there is always room for improvement and growth.	1	2	3	4	5
I prefer to be paid on incentive and am inspired by seeing my income grow along with the business.	1	2	3	4	5
I connect easily with people online and enjoy communicating via telephone, email and instant message.	1	2	3	4	5
I have a suitable home office environment, free of distractions and with all the tools I need to work efficiently.	1	2	3	4	5
I am self-motivated and don't need someone to tell me what to do in order to get the job done.	1	2	3	4	5
I see business as an opportunity for self-growth and expansion.	1	2	3	4	5
I'm inspired when I can buy into the vision and creativity of my clients, taking their ideas and bringing them to life.	1	2	3	4	5
I am tech savvy and understand the systems behind a successful online business.	1	2	3	4	5
I have a high degree of empathy for what it's like to be a creative business owner.	1	2	3	4	5

I know everything is fixable, and look to coach rather than blame when something goes wrong.	1	2	3	4	5
I don't get bogged down by "too many ideas" and can keep projects focused and on task.	1	2	3	4	5
I consistently "unplug" myself and take time outside of my work to spend with family and friends.	1	2	3	4	5

If you scored 1–40

You're not quite there yet. This is a great time to open yourself up to new learning, experience and opportunities, with the possibility of becoming an Online Business Manager in the future. Read on to learn more about this role and see if this is something you may want to work towards.

If you scored 41-70

You have a pretty good foundation for the OBM role; you just need a bit more spit and polish. This book will help you shine a spotlight on the tools that you need to add to your belt before you dive into this role with both feet.

If you scored 71–100

It sounds like you are just steps away from becoming an Online Business Manager. Use the following chapters to clarify what it is you have to offer, what you want to accomplish for your clients (and yourself) and away you go!

② GIVE THEM WHAT THEY WANT

. . . .

WHAT CLIENTS ARE ASKING FOR

The Role of the
Online Business Manager

I like to look at the role of the Online Business Manager through the lens of *how we help support our clients.*

What do clients need? What are they asking for help with (and having trouble finding!)? What is truly going to help them grow and expand their business?

After all, if it wasn't for the needs of our clients, the role of the Online Business Manager wouldn't mean anything. We are here to serve them and their businesses, so it is essential to really understand their needs in order to provide the best level of support.

Together with Andrea Lee, I've spoken to hundreds of small business owners over the past few years who are desperately seeking the help of an Online Business Manager. They didn't know that's what they needed; they just knew they needed help!

Here are some of the most common challenges that people have shared with us:

- "I am so overwhelmed and just can't do this on my own anymore – help!"
- "I'm making a good living, but just can't seem to make my business grow beyond where I am now."
- "I've worked with a bunch of VAs but I can't seem to find one that can do what I need. Why is it so hard to find the right person?"
- "There's so much going on in my business but I'm not sure what is getting done and what isn't. I wish I had someone to manage all those pieces for me."
- "My brain is bursting with new ideas for my business, but I'm busy enough as it is. I guess all these ideas will have to wait ..."

When the client is ready...

In general, clients are ready (and asking!) to hire an OBM when they realize that they can't do it all themselves anymore. Key phrase in that sentence – THEY need to realize it. You may see a client who is struggling with their business because they can't do it all on their own, but if they don't see that and aren't willing to change it then hiring an OBM won't do them a lick of good.

The role of the OBM boils down to one simple thing:

You are freeing up your client so that they can focus their time and energy on the things that only THEY can do in their business.

A question that we recommend all of our clients to ask themselves throughout their work day is:

Is this something only I can do?

If the answer is yes (usually things like setting their vision, marketing, product development and forming and nurturing strategic alliances), we tell them to keep on doing it. If the answer is no, we suggest that it's time for them to let go of that task and pass it on to their team. For many business owners this can be a very tough yet liberating journey. They are used to doing everything on their own, and it takes some time to break the habits of doing the things that really aren't the best use of their time.

And in some cases, the client may even be hiding behind some of these tasks so that they don't have to go out and do the business-building tasks required of them. A client of ours made a point of hiring a bookkeeper for her business, not because she disliked the task but because she enjoyed it! Instead of doing her business-building activities she would distract herself with bookkeeping, and so she hired some-one to take it off her plate and take away her distraction. Very smart.

These distractions are what you can take care of as the OBM. You're not stepping in to do all the work; your role is to manage all the pieces so that the business owner can be free to focus on growth and expansion.

Here is an example of an actual Online Business Manager job description that was originally posted (and filled) in June 2005.

AVAILABLE OPPORTUNITY:
HIRING AN ONLINE BUSINESS MANAGER
OBM #DWSBCOM | June 8, 2005

Multiple Streams of Coaching Income is privileged to assist in the hiring of an Online Business Manager for a six-to-seven figure Online Coach Training and Resource Organization.

We are seeking a bright, dynamic, experienced individual for a long-term contract opportunity with upside compensation potential.

This is a three-quarters to full-time virtual role that is suitable for individuals with fluent spoken and written English in any location including Australia, Canada, UK, USA, etc.

THE ORGANIZATION IN BRIEF

This leading organization has shown double-digit growth in gross revenue over the last 6 months. With more than 15 websites and tens of thousands of online subscribers, its plans to positively support the professional life coach profession are solidly on track.

The organization's core values are contribution, fun

and success and its mission is to **"help the helpers."**
More detailed information about the client company will be provided to short-listed applicants.

This is an excellent opportunity to become a key
player in the growth of a virtual business from a
solid six figures to seven.

ROLE FUNCTION

The Online Business Manager will:

- Have **5+ years experience** in one or more of:
  the fields of marketing, ecommerce, programming, coaching, business management, human
  resources, project management, personal
  development (e.g. Landmark) or other related
  area of study, or equivalent.
- Work with the **very energetic CEO/Owner** of
  the business to create new passive revenue
  streams, taking them from idea to sale
- Manage administration, logistics, human
  resources and infrastructure of a growing
  online business
- **Recruit** additional team members and train/
  manage them into their respective functions
- Be familiar with and/or practically experienced
  in all facets of **Internet marketing** including:

- Product planning and research
- Copywriting
- Website design and creation
- Creation of graphics and user interface
- Product packaging
- Traffic generation
- Conversion and
- The overall strategic marketing plan that creates a cohesive whole out of these elements

• Have experience **creating and implementing a business plan** in a competitive environment

• Be a **relationship builder**, client service oriented and a team player

• Understand **advertising, affiliate programs and joint ventures**; be able to hold and cultivate key relationships

• Diligently maintain and create a standard operating procedure or business training manual for the business

• Be fiscally responsible

In the daily execution of his or her role, the Online Business Manager will use the **Multiple Streams of Coaching Income Product Funnel** model and a number of other approaches to grow the business in alignment with its stated vision and goals for success.

Additional duties may include general email correspondence, telephone communication, engaging in personal learning in the key areas called upon in the role or performing other responsibilities as business need requires.

SKILLS

The Online Business Manager will have the experience and/or aptitude to quickly carry out, or intelligently and economically outsource:

- Website creation
- Graphic creation
- CD/DVD creation
- Typing/transcription/writing/editing/copywriting
- Shopping cart management
- Online list management
- Blog/content management systems
- Hiring and management of multiple contractors in multiple time zones
- Java/php programming
- Project management

Although not mandatory, a thorough understanding of the coaching marketplace, either as trainer, practitioner or business person, is highly desired.

NEXT STEPS/CONTACT INFORMATION

Interested candidates should send their resume/CV to us at xxx [contact information removed] with "OBM #DWSBCOM" in the subject line along with the answers to the questions below. No phone inquiries will be accepted.

If your resume is selected for consideration, we will be in touch via email within 7 days to arrange for the next step in the process.

Thank you in advance for your interest.

Note: Your replies to the below questions are a mandatory part of the consideration process.

1) What websites have you created, or outsourced the creation of, in the past 3 years?
2) What top 3 products, services or other revenue streams have you created or helped create, and what were your approximate revenue goals reached? Provide URLs where appropriate.
3) What is the biggest business opportunity you currently see in either (1) the coaching profession, or (2) the online world?
4) Considering the role in question, what makes you interested in a long-term opportunity

working for someone else, versus growing a business of your own?

5) What are the top 3 characteristics you possess that we should consider when reviewing your application?

We look forward to receiving your application and discovering whether this is your window of opportunity into a new level of wealth, consciousness and joy in your life.

Know of anyone else who would be interested in this opportunity? Please feel free to forward this document to your colleagues.

Is that a job description you would have loved to fill? Great! You'll have a chance to fill that same kind of role for your own clients as an OBM.

Now that you have a general sense of what the Online Business Manager role is, let's go ahead and dive deeper into the specifics.

. . . .

❸ IT ALL STARTS HERE

· ·

THE MARKETING MINDSET

*Clients want someone to brainstorm with,
be proactive and make decisions*

Clients are looking for someone who will treat their business as if it were their own. They realize they can't be everywhere or do everything, but they want the next best thing.

And that's why having a marketing mindset is the foundation of working as an Online Business Manager. It's the one essential skill that is not negotiable.

Deborah Carraro of MyVirtualPartner.com shared a story with me that I think illustrates this beautifully. A couple of years ago, one of her clients moved out of the country. When they got to their new destination they were unable to get an Internet connection for almost four months, which meant that her client had NO way to log in and manage their already successful online business. Deborah stepped in and took over the reins, making sure that her client's business continued to run while they were unavailable. When her client was able to finally get online, everything was still running smoothly and their business continues to grow to this day.

As Deborah says "I treat my client's business as my own – I care whether or not there is a sale that day, whether or not customers are happy. I don't just 'do the tasks' assigned to me, I'm always considering the big picture of their business and how I can help in ways that are beyond what is asked of me."

This is the heart of what the marketing mindset is all about. When working for your clients as OBM, you are truly invested in the growth and success of their business. You look at all aspects of your client's business as though it were your own business.

It's just like someone who is looking for a good daycare

provider for their children. They want someone who will treat their children with love and respect and will also provide an environment in which they can grow and thrive. For clients, their business is their child and a good OBM provides the same loving care.

Know your stuff

The marketing mindset starts with having a **strong understanding of the client's business model.**

You really need to understand how your client makes money. How does their industry work? What are they selling? What is path of their sales funnel from prospect to customer? Who is their target market and what are they doing to reach them?

This comes down to literally being able to *speak the same language* as your client.

After Andrea wrote the book *Multiple Streams of Coaching Income* in 2004, we were constantly approached by clients looking to hire virtual assistants (VAs) and other online support professionals. We quickly started to see a common challenge that many business owners were facing – they were hiring VAs but it wasn't working out.

This was usually for one very simple reason: the virtual

assistant didn't understand what the client was trying to accomplish in their business. They didn't get the "big picture," and as such they had a really hard time providing a thorough level of support for the client's needs. The client would say, "I need to create a pink spoon page," and the virtual assistant would have no idea what they were asking for, let alone how to do it!

In response to this challenge we created the Multiple Streams Team of virtual assistants to provide support to coaches, consultants and other business owners who were creating or growing a business with multiple streams of income. All VAs on the Multiple Streams Team are required to read Andrea's book and understand the concepts. So when a client says to them, "I need to create a pink spoon page," they know that they are referring to a lead generation or "squeeze" page. (The pink spoon page is based on the concept of giving people a "free taste" of what you have to offer, usually in the form of a free report or ecourse, just like a certain ice cream shop gives visitors a sample taste of ice cream on a pink spoon.)

Clients want to hire someone who understands: (1) what they are building in their business and (2) how they are doing it. Sounds so simple at face value, yet it is so very important.

The business model that we recommend and use with

our online business clients is based on the product funnel model, as shown below. This relationship-based business model is an excellent way to build a sustainable and profitable online business. For more information on the product funnel model please see The OBM Toolbox at the back of this book.

FIGURE 3.1 PRODUCT FUNNEL MODEL

Along with the business model you also need to know the **processes involved in implementing the client's various**

marketing and other business-building strategies.

For example, one of the most common marketing strategies in the product funnel is to hold free teleclasses. If your client asked for support with this, would you know all of the elements, steps and information required to setup, promote and execute a successful teleclass?

There's more involved than you may think – here is a sample flowchart of just the first nine steps of the process (for the full chart, see The OBM Toolbox at the end of this book):

Setting Up a FREE Teleclass / Teleseminar

1. The client decides on topic, date, time.	2. Client prepares a summary for the website and email correspondence (this will be used for all pieces - announcement, invitation autoresponder, reminders etc.).	3. VA logs into autoresponder program and creates the autoresponder and sign up form for this teleseminar (includes dial-in, time, summary of topic etc.). For paid calls, create a product.
6. VA double checks links and ensure the sign up form works. Client reviews also.	5. VA updates website or sends appropriate info to web designer to update the website)	4. VA creates sign up form for this teleseminar. VA to confirm what client wants on sign up form (normally just email and name).
7. Client and VA discuss broadcast schedule - when announcements needs to be distributed and to who. - will it be included an ezine?	8. Client/VA brainstorm how to promote teleseminar - submit press release, in ezine, article, joint venture partners etc.	9. VA to monitor sign ups - see how things are going. Respond to inquiries if there are any. Advise client of sign up status.

FIGURE 3.2 SAMPLE FLOWCHART

Your client is looking to you to take care of all of the pieces, whether it's helping them set up a teleclass to creating a sales page for their new book. Even if you outsource the actual work (and I recommend that you do, but we'll talk more about that later), you need to understand and manage the complete process.

What is really required here is **experience**. The best (and probably the only) way to get a strong understanding of online-based business processes is by actually jumping in and doing the work.

I was asked just the other day, "Tina, if I want to work as an OBM, should I first work as a VA so I can gain some experience?" And my answer was a resounding YES!

Go out and start working as a virtual assistant for your ideal clients and within a year or so you could have a strong foundation of experience to start working at the OBM level. Learn about the process of launching a new product. Learn how to research and approach joint venture partners. Learn who to contact if your client wants to create a video promotion. Learn everything that you can!

It's not necessary to have 5-10 years experience before you start working at the OBM level. In fact, most people start to work at the OBM level within 1-3 years of working as a virtual assistant. I know VAs who have reached the "bursting point" within a year and are more than ready to transition to an OBM role (should they wish to do so). For others it may take a few years before they feel they have the experience and confidence to take on this bigger role.

Sidenote

You can never know it all. Online business moves at lightening speed, with constantly changing tools and strategies that no comprehensive training program could ever keep up with. For example, did you know what social networking was a year ago? Or for that matter, do you really understand it now?

I truly believe you can learn just as much working for one year as a virtual assistant as you could learn in four years of business school. The second that someone creates a curriculum for online business training it will be outdated at best (and obsolete at worst). Don't get me wrong, I'm a huge fan of education (having a business degree myself) but when it comes to online business, there is simply no substitute for learning through working.

Therefore I really recommend that you jump in and "ride the wave" of the online world by working in it and by learning great new stuff along the way.

So if you are new to this, go ahead and get started working now as a virtual assistant or in some other online-based role that will get you the experience you need in order to know and understand your clients' online businesses. Or if you have already been working as a VA for a while now, stay up-to-date and remember to keep the end in mind; know that you are working towards something bigger than yourself here, and perhaps bigger than you thought you could be.

A word about training – while there aren't any Online Business Manager training programs out there (yet!), join us at OBMConnect.com where we are gathering the top minds in the VA and OBM industries to learn from each other about the best practices and most effective tools in this ever-changing online world.

OBM as thought partner: Time to speak up!

We all know the value and importance of talking to others about business strategies and ideas. This is the reason people join mastermind groups, hire coaches and create business partnerships. Being a business owner can be a lonely job and I believe it is essential to have others with whom you can collaborate in order to create a successful and fulfilling business.

> ## Sidenote
>
> Having worked from home now since 1999, people often ask me "Aren't you lonely? I think I would get so lonely being at home by myself all day ..." The answer is no, not at all – for the simple fact that almost everything I do is

in collaboration with someone else.

Andrea and I have worked closely together for years on Multiple Streams of Coaching Income, Pink Spoon Marketing, Money Meaning and Beyond and various other projects that are truly to numerous to list here. I also work very closely with Cindy Greenway on Multiple Streams Team and the Hot Skills VA Training programs. Then, of course, there are the many talented and fun clients and contractors that I have the pleasure of working with.

My point here is this: I'm in touch with these people pretty much every day, via email, phone or instant message. So I'm never lonely. In fact, I have forged much stronger relationships online than I ever have working in the offline world. And these relationships are essential to my success – if I had to do it all on my own, it simply wouldn't happen.

Clients want someone to be a sounding board, to brainstorm with them, share ideas and consider options; someone who isn't afraid to speak up. When we talk to business owners, they describe this as their number one wish, "I would love to find someone who will brainstorm with me and help me figure things out." I call it a wish because most business owners have a really hard time finding someone who will do this with them, and have had to "do without" – which means a HUGE opportunity for you!

What is required to be a thought partner? A couple of things; you need both **experience + confidence** in order to be able to effectively speak up with your clients.

Experience comes from having done 'it' before and knowing what's involved with a particular strategy or idea. You can share with your client, "I did X with another client and what happened was Y, so we may want to consider that here." or "I know X tried that once and it really worked, have you also considered doing Y?" The more specific experience we have, the more intelligently and effectively we can contribute to conversations with our clients.

More importantly, you need to **have confidence in yourself, your knowledge and your skill set.** "Getting lippy," with our clients, as I like to call it, does require a bit of sass on your part (heheh)! Some of us have to dig pretty deep to find this confidence; it's a very personal thing. The dictionary defines confidence as, "belief in oneself and one's powers or abilities."

As an OBM, that means that you believe in the value that you have to offer to your client's business. You aren't afraid to speak up and share your ideas, thoughts and experiences with your clients, or more importantly, you ARE afraid and do it anyways.

In my experience, confidence means that you are willing

to contribute without letting the fear or worry of "am I offering value?" get in the way. Or put another way, you are willing to fall flat on your face, get up, shake it off and move on.

The thing is, that will rarely happen.

You see, clients are EAGER to hear from you. They want (and crave!) someone who is willing to engage, brainstorm and share ideas; someone who isn't afraid to challenge them at times, and even say "you are off your rocker here!"; someone who will speak up and tell them what they think (good, bad or otherwise). It is rare that I've heard of someone engaging with their clients at this level and getting put down for it. On the contrary, the clients are usually thrilled to have this kind of input as it is so rare for them.

This doesn't mean that you have to have all the answers (none of us do!). What it does mean is that you are willing to engage, with the intention that 1 + 1 = 3, and that together with your client you can come up with so much more than either of you could ever do alone. THAT is the heart of the OBM relationship.

Sidenote

If the thought of speaking up makes you nervous, I invite you to explore that a bit further.

I find confidence is a cumulative thing, in both life and in business. We all start on the lesser side of confidence, and over time stretch ourselves in various ways that increase our confidence. And the more we stretch, the easier it is to continue to build confidence throughout our lives.

Confidence comes from doing what scares you. So go ahead and open your mouth, especially if the thought of doing so makes you cringe! A good exercise is to think of one of your clients and make a list of ideas that you have for growing their business. Then setup a time to talk with them about your ideas – just say "Sue, I was thinking about your business goals and wanted to share some ideas I had for accomplishing those goals." Most clients will be thrilled that you are thinking about their business growth and will gladly have a conversation with you.

Added value: Always looking for ways to market your client's business

Being that this is the marketing mindset, we naturally want to be looking for ways that we can help to build and grow (market!) our client's business.

The specific strategies will vary depending on the client's overall business plan and niche market. As an OBM you will want to be familiar with and/or practically experienced in all facets of Internet marketing including:

- Product planning and research
- Copywriting
- Website design and creation
- Creation of graphics and user interface
- Product packaging
- Traffic generation
- Conversion and
- The overall strategic marketing plan that creates a cohesive whole out of these elements

You may or may not be the one to actually do some of these marketing activities (depending on your background and strengths), however you DO need to understand Internet marketing and how all the pieces fit together.

As an OBM there are also some more subtle ways to look at

marketing activities.

Whether it's for a specific product or promotion or just throughout the day, I like to ask myself, "What else can we do here?" There are quite often simple little things that can make a big difference in the long run, such as:

- Setting up "Tell a friend" modules on the Thank You page after purchases, so that it is easy for people to send recommendations to their friends
- Implementing an email signature that promotes your clients' free offers and/or products for sale (ensure everyone on the team is using the signatures)
- Creating a digital version of a live event or class to sell separately or as a package
- Adding an effective P.S. at the bottom of a sales page
- Making the Buy buttons on a sales page extra attractive and noticeable
- Creating an upsell on the order page for a product, for example, "Buy this book together with our workbook and save 15%"
- Putting a little extra "oomph" and adding keywords into the title of an article
- Introducing clients to each other so they can cross-promote
- Being on the lookout for new easy places to promote, advertise or find joint venture partners
- Adding more autoresponder messages that follow up

with previous customers so they are reminded to visit your client's offerings again

Calling the shots: Being a decision maker for the business

On a day-to-day basis there are many decisions to be made in any online based business: When do we want to send out this promotion? Who is going to fix the typo on our website? Where can we find someone to edit my book? How should I respond to this upset customer? What should our next new product offering be?

Without an OBM, the majority of these decisions fall squarely on the shoulders of business owners. As such, anytime there is a question, their team members will turn to them for the answer. Because most business owners are incredibly busy, this process results in delays and it can also feel like a hassle to have to deal with every little thing.

That's why our clients want someone who is willing and able to make decisions on their behalf, and not wait to run everything past them first. This doesn't mean that you will be making ALL decisions for your client, however you can certainly help with a lot of the tactical and operational decisions that come up on a day-to-day basis.

How do you know when you should check with your client before making a decision?

Generally, any decisions about money or strategy should be run by your client. On the other hand, your client will probably be relieved once you take over some of the administrative, operational and customer service decisions. When you first start working with a new client, you will run a lot of things by them, as you get to know each other and build a level of trust that will give you more freedom in making decisions down the road.

You may also want to set some standards and procedures around this. For example, I once worked with a client whose policy was that her team could make a decision on refunds that would be less than $100, but anything over $100 had to be brought to her attention. A "Decision Making Standards" guide can be something that you create for your client, and add to over time as reference for future decisions.

When you do need to approach your client for a decision, come to them with a proposed solution.

Let's say that you have an angry customer email that you aren't quite sure to handle. Instead of asking your client, "How do you want me to respond to this?" craft a potential response to the customer and send it to your client, asking,

"I'm not quite sure how to respond to this. Will you check my proposed response below and let me know if this is OK or if you have changes?" Not only will your client love you for being proactive, you will also speed up the decision-making process as your client can review and respond much quicker than they can create their own response from scratch.

Be your client's personal first line of defense

Your job as the OBM is also to protect your client from certain decisions that your client should not be wasting his or her time on. This is especially important with operational and systems-based decisions.

Let's say your client wants to set up a new blog-based website. First, bring them a summary of options and ideas for them to consider and ask for their approval on the parameters of the project. While you are creating the blog, do NOT go to them with every little question that you have ("Where do you want your RSS feed link? Did you want me to add your picture here? Should I change this description to match your main website?").

Instead, go ahead and set up the new blog based on your experience and then have your client look at a draft version and request any changes. Again, it is better to present them with a solution to review (a completed draft version of the blog) than to ask them what to do at every step along the way.

This is ESPECIALLY important for clients who actually enjoy systems and administrative tasks. If given the chance, these clients can very easily become involved in these things to the point of distraction. These clients may want to know more about the details than other clients would, but don't be afraid to lovingly "slap their wrist" if they try to become too involved. It is not the best use of their time to get too involved on the backend and you may need to remind them of that.

Becoming a part of the client's business

I have a coaching client who has been in business for over four years now, and has a number of people on her team who have worked with her that entire time. We were talking recently about ways that she can get out of the day-to-day needs of her business so she can focus more on growth activities. I asked about the current people on her team and whether any of them might be ready to take on a bigger role within her business. Her response:

> *"There is one girl I've worked with for years who does a great job, but she always refers to it as 'your business.' For example she will say 'Here is an update for YOUR webpage' or 'What do YOU want to do here.' Never does she say OUR, US or WE when talking about the work we do together, even after all these years. So I don't get the sense that she really cares about my business"*

71

Can you see what my client is saying here? The words that her team member is using are drawing a line between her client's business and the work she is doing for her client. She isn't really showing that she is engaged or invested in the work.

This is such an interesting distinction! On one hand I totally get why this is happening – after all, it isn't the team members business, so why should she act as though it is? This is how most contractors (and employees) act with our clients (and employers). We draw a line in the sand between the two of us, and I believe that's in order to keep ourselves safe from the impact our work has on our client's business.

We're not going to get deep into the psychology of why this happens, but I would really like to challenge this status quo way of working.

When a client hires us to work with them and contribute to their business is some way, it truly is a collaborative effort. Whether it's doing their filing or helping them create a new product line, the end result is created together. While the client may own that result, energetically you are a part of it as well.

Take a look at the words you use when talking to or about your clients. Are you saying YOURS or OURS? YOU or WE? Pay attention to what you are saying or typing over the next few days, and make note of it.

I challenge you to start using more inclusive language and pay attention to how that feels. Does it make you uncomfortable? If so, dig a little bit into that and see what's up. Perhaps you need to do a bit of personal work to feel comfortable with this level of engagement. It could be you feel you don't deserve it, or perhaps you truly don't have confidence in the work you do. Or maybe there is an issue with the client that you need to face. This can be a tough process indeed, but don't be afraid to shine that light on what is going on behind the scenes.

Being plugged in as a part of your client's business is absolutely essential to working in a OBM capacity. If you aren't able to do that then this may not be the best role for you.

(4) # WHAT SETS YOU APART

A COACHING APPROACH

*It's not always about what you do,
but how you do it.*

*There is a subtle skill in working as an OBM that will really
help you connect and grow with your clients, what we call the
Coaching Approach. I consider Andrea to be one of the finest
coaches that I know, and was quite thrilled when she agreed to
write this chapter! So allow me to pass the mic to Andrea here
for a short while.*

When Tina asked me to contribute this chapter to her book,
I had to smile to myself a little. Little did she know how
much of what I'd write would be a direct result of my expe-

e brings to the world: stellar, steadfast and
ning business management of the online
collaborated on for more than eight years.
It's little wonder that we now call each other the best of
possible business partners and once-in-a-lifetime friends.

There is a simple example that will begin to show you why
this chapter is an important part of this book, and it has to
do with things going wrong. Although the rest of this book
will, I believe, become a textbook for the ages to guide you
through the new territory of online business management,
there are still, to be blunt, a lot of potential pitfalls you will
want to be on the alert for.

Which is where a so-called "coaching approach" comes in,
and it will be especially useful to you for the very reason
that there are so many unknowns on planet OBM.

So just what is this thing we're calling a coaching approach?
Consider this:

> *You are an Online Business Manager for an industry
> leader who's got some very big business growth in the
> works. One of their key projects has you in charge of
> a team of two virtual individuals. One of them, let's
> call her Randy, had a deadline last week that she hasn't
> met. She's been saying she's on top of it but you're getting
> a wonky feeling about it – it doesn't smell right to you.*

Turns out, you're right. You use your project management, operations management and people management skills (that you will be learning about in the next chapters) and sort out that basically, Randy has dropped the ball big time. The work isn't done.

But even worse than that, she's led you to believe it's been fine the whole time when the fact of the matter is, she was stuck, didn't ask for help, and let things get completely out of hand before "fessing up" when you confronted her. She probably didn't even understand what was required of her in the first place. Not a pretty sight, and in some ways, something that can only happen this drastically because of the online nature of the team. In other words, the kind of mess an OBM can either sink or swim in.

You know the kind of the cleanup they have to do at the fish market after a busy morning? Yep. Bad.

So as the Online Business Manager in this scenario, what do you do? You have any number of choices available – what does your instinct tell you? Take a moment to listen in to your rational mind telling you, "I'd do step one, two and then three," while your emotions are saying "Oh, crap."

The coaching approach aside for the moment, clearly you will have some concrete, nuts and bolts things to do, just as any manager would – whether they are in HR for a law firm or the head server at a pub. What's the extent of the damage? Does the person need to be taken off the project, rapido, or will you have them clean it up? How is your client impacted and can they immediately be cared for and retained? Who on the team could step up into the situation and pinch hit?

You need to go beyond the practical

The heart of a coaching approach goes beyond all these reasonable and practical management skills. It goes to the idea that wherever something great is being achieved, a coaching approach is in there somewhere. And that wherever a coaching approach is used, a greater degree of success will follow.

Coaching is ...

A questioning approach towards thinking, living and communicating that improves everything.

Applying the coaching approach to our fish market scenario, after the dust has settled it might look like this:

COACHING APPROACH TACTIC #1: Assume everyone is doing their very best, especially when they don't seem like it.

This means that even though the Virtual Assistant crashed and burned, there is a story behind it. Not even just that their dog is ill, or they're overworked, either. Very often it can mean that (1) expectations of the project weren't clear in the beginning (2) they did not realize they were welcome to ask "stupid" questions (3) prior experience on projects for this business had deadlines that were flexible or even (4) their self-esteem is low for unrelated reasons and they aren't good at setting personal boundaries or saying no.

COACHING APPROACH TACTIC #2: Set up a business culture that requires over-communication, always. And that the only real mistake that can occur is the failure to communicate early.

In an online business situation, the majority of unknown "gotcha's" will be prevented with the application of this one coaching approach tactic. I've been known to get very adamant when emphasizing this one, along the lines of:

"You can't get it wrong UNLESS you don't tell me you're getting it wrong." Translation? **The only real mistake is a failure to communicate**. You can call me up in the middle of the night and tell me things are doing horribly, and really, I will be much more okay with it than not knowing until it's too late.

COACHING APPROACH TACTIC #3: Be serenely confident in the fact that until you successfully go through

a conflict or sensitive negotiation with someone, you don't know the true nature of the relationship.

I am of the conviction that until you have to go through a tough or even just touchy something with someone, you aren't really friends. Perhaps because Tina and I only ever work with clients we respect as much as our friends, we apply this to our business relationships too.

As an OBM who's in it for the long haul, and wants to really reach the pinnacle of success available, be open and willing to embrace conflict. Take feedback as a vitamin and strengthen your internal self each time. Use the other coaching approach tactics here to anchor your conflict in productive conversation. Remember that to the degree you can be serene through a conflict, the more you are learning and the less likely you'll have to go through this same conflict again, in another form.

How does this apply in our scenario? In mentoring OBMs over the years, we've come to recognize that managing conflict is one of the most difficult things an OBM does. Your goal is to be able to transcend the fear of initiating, quickly, the conversations that need to happen with the errant VA and also of presenting the ugly problem to your client.

COACHING APPROACH TACTIC #4: Come to understand that the business can only grow to the extent, and at

the rate that, the business owner grows as a person.

I call this the "Paul Principle," in sharp contrast to the "Peter Principle" which says that in corporations, people will rise to the level of their incompetency and then stay there. Likewise, in any given business, the growth of the business will rise or fall to the level of the business owner's personal development. If a business owner isn't willing to look themselves in the mirror and acknowledge their whole selves, experience says the business won't be able to make big shifts either.

Applying this once again to our scenario, let's use our imaginations to illustrate this tactic.

Is it possible that the business owner has made a habit of requesting to start lots of new projects at the last minute, within short timeframes, only to abandon them later, making deadlines moot (and downright annoying)?

Is it possible the business owner "owed" something to the virtual assistant and didn't follow through, preventing the VA from being able to proceed and leaving the VA feeling unable to speak "truth to power" out of fear?

Could we consider the fact that the business owner is someone of such high profile that the VA has put herself in a state of ultra-sensitivity, worrying about her performance and in awe about her association with this person, resulting in her being paralyzed and stuck?

Especially when it comes to the online world, these are the subtexts that can often emerge ONLY when a coaching-approach is taken. Based on the scenario and tactics above, I hope you're beginning to grasp what it means to take a coaching approach as an Online Business Manager. It can be boiled down to something very simple:

It's not only what you do but HOW you do it that will set you apart.

So how do you translate this into the way of being that is the heart of what an Online Business Manager is?

There's no requirement that you become a coach or take coach training, however if you do it will without question better equip you for your OBM career as well as transform your life. Start with the basic tenet that underlines everything coaching:

Questions.

Lead with questions.

In case of emergency, ask the very best questions you have.

Ask what questions you're not asking and what those will reveal.

Which brings us to...

COACHING APPROACH TACTIC #5: Recognize that a business is one of the world's most effective vehicles for personal transformation there is.

As an Online Business Manager the trials and tribulations you go through as you invest in the vision of your clients will coach you, if you let them.

One of your clients is taking a sabbatical for three months and you will earn considerably less. Have you become a little complacent about your work as an OBM and what will this 3-month window allow you to do, or become, as a person and a professional?

The business is taking a new turn and you don't have the specialized expertise required. Is this an opportunity for you to release your preference to be the one who knows everything? Can your identity as a success survive the fact that you won't be the smart one in this scenario?

You're in a low energy mood for a while and you realize it's because you're tired of using a coaching approach with your client! Instead, you turn it on yourself and ask yourself where are you not stretching?

The ways in which a coaching approach can be applied to your path as an OBM are limitless. In fact, I would encourage you not to think of a coaching approach as something you turn on and off, or as a blanket you put on top of something. It's the inner fuel that drives the work, not decoration.

As you read on in the chapters that follow, I know you'll benefit beyond measure from what is provided as concrete direction for how to play a bigger role with your clients and yourself. Read and listen closely and you'll see a coaching approach between the lines, and that this theme runs as a thread throughout the OBM conversation. In fact, I'll go so far as to say that quite possibly, without a coaching approach to business, the OBM role would not have emerged quite this way!

The very best OBMs are an embodiment of the coaching approach and speaking as a business owner, I'm incredibly grateful for this.

I hope you don't mind if I say on behalf of the business owners whose lives and business you will touch, thank you, for your willingness to wade into these uncharted waters.

You're about to enter into the guts of the "doing" part of the book, where the "what you do" steps are revealed. As you soak in the wisdom there, read with a coaching approach in mind. And when you're ready to apply a coaching approach in real-life, here are some sample questions you can refer back to:

- As we talk about X (where X is a new project, idea, problem that needs solving), what happens in your physical body?
- Why do you think X is happening? (Where X is a recurring problem, results that aren't as stellar as hoped, an emotional reaction on the part of the client)
- Would you prefer to earn more money and work a little more, or earn about the same amount of money and work a lot less?
- What is the end goal of your business – is it to work it until you retire at a certain time? Sell it to someone for a lump sum? Have it be run by a team while you pursue other interests?
- What other area of your life have you experienced success in? What can you transfer from that success and apply to your business? (A person trained in martial arts might recognize they aren't being as strict or disciplined with themselves in their business as they can be, and can enjoy being.)

⑤ DRIVING THE BUS

· ·

PROJECT MANAGEMENT

*Clients want someone to help ensure
that things get done*

As a business grows, it becomes more and more important to have someone who is staying on top of everything to make sure it gets done (this person is traditionally called a project manager in a corporate business setting).

According to Wikipedia, *project management* is the **discipline** of **planning, organizing, and managing** resources to bring about the successful completion of specific project goals and objectives.

Many business owners are horrible project managers (or they really don't enjoy it). They started their business because they wanted to offer their expertise to the world, not so they could run a business. So they are either tolerating a role that they really don't like doing or they are having a hard time getting things done at all. They want and need someone to come in and take control of the various projects and elements of their business, to ensure that things run smoothly and get done in a timely matter.

I like to call this **driving the bus**. It is our clients who determine where the bus needs to go (the end result you are working towards), but it up to the OBM to make sure that we get there.

With this role you are taking a huge load off the client's shoulders. They no longer need to be the one to constantly manage all the people and tasks involved in completing projects. Instead, **they can focus their time and energy on the things that only THEY can do.** This is the ultimate goal of the OBM!

Your responsibility here is simple – get stuff done! I can't tell you how many times I've spoken to business owners who have loads of projects in various stages of completion that are just sitting there and rotting away, for the simple fact that they are either too busy or too distracted to see things through to the end. It's literally like a goldmine hiding just a foot under the ground, ready for someone to discover it and bring it's wealth to the world.

That's why a good OBM truly is "worth their weight in gold" to the client.

Sidenote

I take a very simple view of project management. An 'official' overview of project management would go into much more than I cover here – milestones, Gantt charts and such. These things honestly make my head spin, and while necessary in the huge projects that corporations tackle, I have yet to need them myself.

To me the heart of project management is "getting stuff done in the simplest way possible." Sometimes the more complex philosophies, steps and tools can get in the way of that and create a new pile of work themselves. There is certainly nothing wrong with using project management methodologies and tools, just be sure that they are actually helping projects move forward and not causing confusion or delay.

Are project managers born or created?

Ahhh, the age old question of nature or nurture. I'm certainly not claiming to have an answer, just a perspective.

From what I've seen, some people are really good at project management; usually those who are naturally organized, able to 'see all the pieces' and have a track record of moving things along to completion. Other people may fall flat. They may be good at getting their own stuff done, but not good at pulling together all the people and pieces required to get a bigger project done.

How do you know if you're a good project manager? Take on a project and see if it gets done. The proof is in the pudding, as they say.

In some cases you may just need some more experience to hone your project management skills; with a few projects under your belt you could become an excellent project manager. It's like you have a dormant gene that – once activated – kicks into high gear and away you go.

The key quality of a good project manager is that they don't shy away from the responsibility. They are willing to take on a project and know that they are accountable for whether or not it gets done. They need to be energized by this responsibility, not paralyzed by it (though a bit of fear is OK, so long as it motivates you in a positive way).

Let's take a closer look at what exactly project management is:

Discipline

Discipline – how I love that word. At face value it sounds almost harsh and punitive, but in my mind discipline means honouring a commitment. If you say you are going to do something, then you do it. You own the responsibility of getting something done. It's up to you.

This is where most projects fall apart. After all, it can be really easy to plan something, organize and even get started. However, without discipline it can be just as easy to let things slide and never reach completion.

In best practices you really do need to **have one person be the project manager** – not having a designated "owner" for a project generally means that it won't get done. I've seen it time and time again. There may be plenty of people on the bus, but no one is driving it.

This happens a lot in small business teams, for the simple fact that so many of us are used to working alone and doing everything ourselves.

Planning

Before starting any project you want to make sure you plan before you start. This is SO important in order to prevent frustration and wasted time and resources along the way.

Let's look at an example. Your client has just written a book and needs to get a sales page "live" so he can start selling the book.

The first step is to plan the sales page, which means getting really clear on what exactly your client wants.

- Is there an example of a sales page that he really likes? Which elements does he like or not like? I always like to work from an example, especially if your client is new to sales pages or really wants to try something different.
- Does he want a short/sweet style sales page or a longer/harder sell page?
- What domain name does he want for the sales page?
- Will you need to hire a copywriter to write the page?
- Do you need a 3D graphic of the book to put on the page?
- What look (colours, graphics, layout) does he want for the page?
- Does he have testimonials ready or do you need to collect some?
- What price will the book sell for? Is it an e-book or print book?
- Are there any bonuses to go along with the purchase?
- Is there going to be a special launch price/offer?
- Does your client want an upsell as part of the buying process (e.g., Buy the book and workbook for a discounted price)

As you can see, in order to effectively plan this project, you need to have a strong understanding of all the elements of setting up a sales page. If you don't have experience in this yet, then I suggest finding a few sales pages and studying each element of the page.

You will also want to consider the cost of each piece of the project so that you can a) have a good idea of what the overall cost will be, b) prevent last minute surprises and c) have a guideline for keeping costs in check.

Organizing

You've planned out the project and all the requirements, now it's time to start organizing all the pieces. In the online business world this generally means that you will be hiring contractors to complete various parts of the project. In our sales page example, you may need:

- A copywriter to create the words
- A graphic designer to create a header and/or 3D graphic of the book
- A web designer or techie VA to actually create the page
- A VA to set up the Buy button and link it to the shopping cart
- A VA to coordinate collection of testimonials and bonus items.

Of course there may be certain elements that you are going to do yourself, as well.

You will also want to have a timeline for when you need each element completed, so you can coordinate with vendors on when you need their piece completed. For example, you will need the copywriter and designer to be finished before the web designer can create the page. Check The OBM Toolbox at the back of this book for a list of online project management tools that you can use to map out your process and track everything.

Managing

You've laid the foundation (planning) and organized all of your resources (people); now it's time to get to work. This is where the management piece comes in, which is perhaps the most important part of the process.

When people ask me what I do for a living I like to joke and say, "I'm a professional nag," but in some ways I'm not really joking. This is where I spend a lot of my energy day-to-day – checking in with people to ensure that their part of the project is moving along and will be completed on time (or not, in which case I need to make adjustments around that).

I've found that most people need a bit of a "loving nag" from time to time to get stuff done. It's just human nature;

if we don't have someone stressing the importance of getting X done (nagging us), then it can be very easy for us to let X slide a bit and not complete it. This is especially important when working with contractors who have a bunch of different clients and projects on the go. Think about it – if you have four design projects on your plate and you KNOW that I'm going to be asking you for mine (versus another client who may not nag quite so much), whose project are you going to work on first? Probably mine, so you can get me out of your hair, heheh.

I think we assume that people will get stuff done when they say they will, but this isn't always true. It's not that people are bad or lazy. In fact it's usually quite the opposite with most contractors that I've had the pleasure to work with. They are SO busy that they have a hard time getting everything done in the time that they promised. They don't mean to be late with a project; they are just struggling to complete something for you and 10 other people at the same time. Well, as the saying goes – the squeaky wheel gets the grease – so I'm certainly not shy when it comes to checking in with them and "nagging" a bit as needed.

How do you nag? It's simple, really. If I want to check-in with a contractor on the status of a project, I will send an email that says something like:

Hi Ben,

Just checking on the status of the 3D book graphic you are working on for us. Do you have a draft ready for our review?

Thanks!

Or if it was due yesterday and I haven't received it yet, I might say:

Hi Ben,

Just checking on the status of the 3D book graphic you are working on for us. You were going to have it ready for us yesterday. If you already sent it over I may have missed that email, do you mind resending?

If it's not ready yet, can you give me an ETA on completion? As you know, we have a designer starting on the sales page tomorrow and we need to have the graphic ready by then.

Thanks!

It is especially important to not let emotions come into play here, even when you are feeling frustrated because someone is late with something or if you've emailed them five times and aren't getting an answer. People will usually respond in kind, so if you get nasty with them chances are they will get nasty with you. And when that happens, I can almost guarantee that your projects will fall to the bottom of their list.

Remember, being late usually isn't anything personal; it's just a result of the contractor being overwhelmed with work themselves. A little compassion can go a long way. If I know that a contractor is really struggling with everything on their plate and I have some "wiggle room" on my end, I like to be able to take a bit of pressure off for them.

Suzy, I know you are swamped right now. We are OK to wait until Friday for the new banner if that helps. Let me know, thanks!

It's this kind of consideration that will pay dividends in the long run, as you build strong relationships with your contractors and stay at the top of their list for future projects.

The key to nagging is to do it! Check in with people on a regular basis (daily is good, hourly is too much). If it's super important I may even send a second email later in the day if they haven't responded to an earlier message that I sent. And if I'm really desperate I'll pick up the phone and call (which I rarely have to do).

Sidenote

Andrea has an excellent strategy that she uses when she is waiting get a response from someone, what I like to call her "bait and catch" strategy. She will send someone a really simple request via email, something like "Which of these graphics do you prefer?" When she gets a response to that simple email it's a signal that the person is online now, so she quickly sends another email about a matter she's been waiting for an answer about.

She has "caught" the person online, the virtual equivalent of catching someone in their office. The person can't simply brush off her email and pretend that they aren't online. Quite often she will finally get a response to the other matter she has been waiting on, for the simple fact that they can't hide from her at that moment.

Or, better yet (sneaky her), sometimes she even puts two items into one email. One item is something she knows the person will reply to, something juicy like a win or celebration, and the other item is the request. Hey, whatever works that's civilized and respectful is okay in my books.

The key here is that your "bait" email is very simple, something they can read and respond to right away. If you send a bait email that is more than a quick read, then chances are they will just let it sit in their Inbox along with your other requests. In fact, you'll learn very quickly that short emails are the way to go overall.

Three strikes and you're out!

If you don't get a response after three tries within three days then I would look for someone else to complete that task for you. It's one thing for someone to be running late and let you know about it, it's a whole other thing to be ignored. I won't tolerate that and I will quickly cut those contractors loose.

Clients need nagging too

Don't be afraid to nag your clients too! Most of my clients really want me to nag them to get things done, and in fact I've been hired by some people for just this reason. As one client so delicately put it, "Tina, I know that you are like a bulldog with a bone – you just don't let go. And I need someone like that to keep me on task." Strange as it may seem, this was quite a compliment in my books, heheh.

Sometimes our client can be the biggest barrier to getting a project complete, except now we can't use the three strikes rule (LOL). You can nag your clients, of course, but here are three other things you can do to make projects easier for them to complete.

1. Start it for them

Working with Andrea, this is probably one of the things I do the most. I'll get something started for her – usually a writing project of some kind – and then she'll take it from there and tweak or edit as she sees fit. It is scientifically proven that starting something is what requires the most energy, but that once you get going it doesn't take near as much energy to keep going. Your clients are busy enough; get their project started and it will take a lot less of their time and energy to take it through to completion.

For example, I will quite often create a draft of Andrea's online newsletter *Creating What Matters* and she will then take it and edit it as she likes. The funny thing is, quite often she will pretty much change everything I sent to her in the first place, almost like she had created it from scratch anyhow! But while it may almost seem like I didn't really help, in reality it was the act of "getting it started" that helped the most.

Sidenote

Don't get offended if your client takes a writing project that you start and totally changes it. This generally isn't a reflection of the quality of your work, it is more to do with the client wanting to write "in their own voice," or that they have simply decided to talk about something else. It's never personal, so don't take it to heart. And just the same way that a married couple starts to finish each other's sentences over time, you will soon be able to write in your client's voice without even thinking about it.

2. Ping-pong it

If your client has started something and is stuck with it, ask them if you can take a stab at it for them. Sometimes a fresh eye and new perspective is all that is needed to get something done. You can take a look at what they've done so far, add your bit to it and send it back to them to jump into again. This may go back and forth a few times, which is why we call it the ping-pong strategy. This is a HIGHLY effective way to get the momentum going on something that is just sitting there stuck for whatever reason.

3. Ask them what they need

I've found that sometimes a task may not be complete for the simple fact that the client needs something in order to finish it, and they are either too busy or distracted to remember that they can ask for your help.

For example, your client may be working on a Welcome letter for a sales page, and they want to quote something from a book they read recently but can't find the book on their shelf. You could easily do a bit of research and find the quote for them so they can get it done. When you do a little bit of digging you may find that your client is stuck by something that could be easily handled on your end, and you are able to quickly fix it so they can keep on moving.

BECOMING AN ONLINE BUSINESS MANAGER

Helping them to let go

"People do what they do because they have nothing more compelling to do." • THOMAS LEONARD

Most business owners are used to doing everything themselves, and there are some that may have a tough time letting go of making sure that things get done. They may be constantly looking over your shoulder, asking for updates on every little piece, wanting to approve each step and essentially driving you nuts!

When you are new to working with a client or to doing a particular project for them then it is certainly natural for them to be more closely involved; essentially there is a training process going on. But there comes a time when the client needs to step back and let you do what they've hired you to do. Otherwise the work will be highly frustrating for you, and it can make it really tough for you to get any work done.

When you first start working with a client they may have **Lone Ranger Syndrome.**

Even though they very clearly want and need help in the management and completion of projects, they are used to being intimately involved and may find it tough to not be plugged into the process. They are used to being a Lone

Ranger in their business and knowing everything that is going on, and they are finding it a hard habit to break.

Lone Rangers generally just need some time to build trust in you – they need to see that you can create results so that they can let go of the need to "know it all." If you simply do your job and understand your client's need to check in on your results, then over time they will get less and less involved as they trust that you will handle things. Some clients may end up with a bunch of free time that they don't know what to do with, and it's your job to gently remind them to work on business-building activities, the things that they wished they had time to do before you came along; anything that only THEY can do.

If your client gets really stuck in this space you may want to suggest that they hire a business coach to help them decide where to best focus their time and energy in this stage of business growth.

If you have worked together for a while and your client is still not letting go then you may have a **Control Freak** on your hands.

At first you may not be able to tell that a client is a Control Freak, but it will become clear after you've proven yourself several times to be competent, yet they still want to be involved in every little thing. I would suggest that you first have a conversation with your client, and simply point out that they've hired you to do this job for them and it is not the best use of their time to still be so involved.

If things don't change after having this conversation, then this could be a VERY tough situation to work with as an OBM, as you will essentially be doing double-duty of managing all of the pieces and keeping your client updated on all the pieces as well.

In our experience there isn't much you can do to change this in your client, as it is usually something quite deeply ingrained and beyond the scope of an OBM to handle or fix. You may very well have to cut them loose at some point; it is near impossible to truly help someone take their business to the next level when they aren't willing to let go. Save your gifts for those who will use them.

. . . .

⑥ STREAMLINE AND SIMPLIFY

· ·

OPERATIONS MANAGEMENT

Clients want someone to setup systems that ensure their business runs smoothly

One of the keys to growth is to set up a strong foundation of business systems and standards. Without it a business can only grow so far, and may in fact fall apart like a deck of cards.

I'm reminded of a fulfillment house that we used to use for all of our book shipments. When we first started using them they were a smaller company, the type where you could phone and it would actually be the owner who answered your call. As time went on we could see that they were becoming busier and growing by leaps and bounds. Then, suddenly one day they shut down – no warning, just an email that stated they were no longer in business.

What happened? From what we could tell they had simply grown too fast, and their infrastructure couldn't handle it. Such a shame really, when any business owners dream is to keep on growing. But without a strong foundation, that growth may turn into a nightmare.

This is where the OBM comes in, ensuring that all business systems, procedures and tools are in place and functioning smoothly to the benefit of the business.

Standard operating procedures

A great starting point is to help your clients put together a Standard Operating Procedures guide (what we like to call a SOP). As a business grows, it is essential to have a central how-to guide for handling everything that needs to be done. How are orders processed? What are the proper responses to various customer service enquiries? Where are the websites hosted and how do you update the sites?

We highly recommend using an online tool such as PBWiki. com to create an SOP. This will give everyone a central, online location for accessing the guide when needed (versus having a Word document that lives on someone's computer). Plus, a wiki system is very easy to update and will track when changes are made and by whom. PBWiki.com also has a great notification system and will send everyone an email update when something is new or changed (so you don't have to send updates manually).

Here is a screenshot of the SOP Guide for Multiple Streams of Coaching Income:

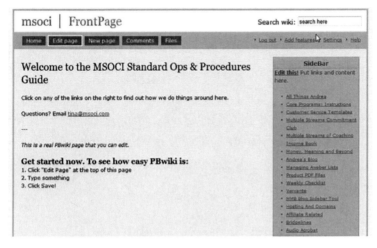

FIGURE 6.1 SCREENSHOT OF SOP

Creating an SOP is a great first OBM project with your clients. Most small business owners don't have an SOP in place. They understand the importance of having such a guide, especially as they grow and continue to bring more people onto their team. However they haven't had the time or inclination to put one together themselves (for most business owners this would be a daunting task, nor is it the best use of their time). So having someone take on the task of creating an SOP is a huge relief to them.

Really, a business is not grown up until they have an SOP in place – it is that important to a growing business and thus a worthy project for any OBM to tackle. The SOP becomes your touchstone for success in the area of operations. As the business grows you always want to ensure that you have the latest systems in place AND that they are being tracked and managed via the SOP.

Automate, automate, automate

When a business owner wants to expand his or her business the first thing they usually think of is growing their team. This is certainly part of growth and we will discuss expanding the team in our next chapter.

But before doing any hiring you need to first take a look at the client's business systems and processes. Chances are that there are some things that you would hire for that could be automated instead.

I recommend automating over hiring any day for a few reasons:

- Automating a process means less room for errors and delays.

- You will generally pay less for an automated system than you will for a person to do the same task.
- Automating certain tasks (especially tedious tasks) frees up the team to focus on other business building tasks – a benefit to both the client and the team members (who may be getting bored with these types of tasks).

For example, Andrea and I recently made a change to how we process orders for our print book *Money, Meaning and Beyond*.

Our old system required that we purchase a bunch of books up front and ship them to our fulfillment warehouse for storage. Then, as orders were processed in our shopping cart system our VA would export those orders and then manually upload them to the fulfillment house once a week for shipping.

Then we switched to using a "print on demand" supplier for our book, which has made this whole process much easier. Thanks to the wonderful folks at Vervante.com, we now have an automated system that connects directly to our shopping cart. Now, when a book order comes into our cart it is set to notify Vervante to produce a book and ship it out. There is no need for our VA to do anything at all anymore, nor any delays on shipping or missed orders as everything happens automatically with each order. So nice!

The three key benefits of this change have been:

- We save the upfront cost of maintaining a stock of print books.
- We save the cost to store those books at a fulfillment warehouse.
- We no longer have to rely on our VA to process the orders for shipping; everything happens automatically between our shopping cart and Vervante, even if our VA is sick or on holidays.

See how a simple, automated system can make a big difference? We actually need to use our VA LESS, resulting in lower costs and higher profit with less work. Now that's the power of automation at work.

Check The OBM Toolbox at the back of this book for a list of recommended tools and systems.

How do you decide what to automate in your client's business? Here are some questions that will help:

What 'tedious' tasks are your clients and/or their team spending a lot of time on?

I find that the tedious tasks are usually the ones that are easiest to automate. Article submission is a good example. Most clients want to do some form of article marketing, and will quite often delegate this task to a VA on their team. Depending on how many sites they are submitting to, submitting one article can take a VA up to five hours or more! Plus, most VAs really don't enjoy this task, and it will quite often fall to the bottom of their list and in some cases not get done at all.

There are some great article submissions systems available now that will automate this process for you. You just enter your article once and these systems blast out that article to a bunch of sites. This frees your VA to focus on other business-building activities for you.

It is especially important to see what kinds of tedious tasks your client is doing themselves. Again, we want to always be trying to take things off our clients' plates so they can focus on the more important business-building activities that only THEY can do.

I recently started working with a client who was manually entering names into her newsletter database from an online free quiz that she offers. Eek! First of all, she shouldn't be the one entering those names into the newsletter database; her VA should be doing that for her. And more importantly, this could easily be an automated process. So now we're setting up the online form to send this information directly to the newsletter database as soon as someone takes the quiz – no fuss, no muss!

Are there ongoing errors or delays occurring anywhere in your business?

One of my clients ran a 6-month coaching program and asked each member of the program to read and agree to a set of standards to complete their registration. She would send a PDF form for her coaching clients to print, read, sign and fax back. Then, a VA would gather the faxes, enter the client contact information into a spreadsheet and send the client a Welcome package. This was a lot of work for the VA to coordinate, and also created a gap between when a person would send in their fax and when they would receive their Welcome packet (sometimes a day or so, depending on how busy the VA was).

To simplify the process, we set up an online agreement form. Now, when someone registers for the program they are taken to a webpage with an online agreement form that they can immediately read and "sign" (by submitting their name). Once they submit their name, they gain immediate access to the online Welcome packet. What was a 7-step and labour-intensive process that took two days or more, is now a simple, three-step process that takes minutes and is easier for everyone involved.

Put yourself in your customer's shoes and ask: is there anything in your buying process that could be simpler, quicker or more pleasant?

As we got a glimpse of in the last example, automated systems can also make it much easier for customers to engage with your client, which is VERY important for the success of their business. You want to make it very easy for customers to buy, and automated systems will make the buying process smooth and enjoyable for all concerned.

I'm sure you have come across a situation similar to this – you are on a website and like what they have to offer. You go to click the Buy button and on the next page you're directed to print out an order form and fax it in, or to call in your order.

Now I don't know about you, but in most cases they have just lost my sale (unless I REALLY want what they have to offer). I don't want to spend the time to print out a form, fill it in by hand, fax it in and wait to get a response or confirmation of my order. Nor do I want to pick up the phone and wait for service or delay my order because I'm surfing in the off hours (as I often do). I'm ready to make my purchase now, and would willingly submit my credit card number to do it. I want to order and pay and get immediate confirmation of my order. And in the case of downloadable products, I want instant access.

The more steps you ask a potential client to take in order to purchase, the less likely they will be to complete the sale. So look to automate and simplify the buying process as much as possible. An online shopping cart system is a definite must if you are selling online.

In a nutshell the name of the game is simple:

Is there a better way to do this?

This isn't just a one-time thing; it is something that you will always be doing as an OBM. In fact, you may want to commit to reviewing your entire Standard Operating Procedures guide at least once a year – we call this a Better Way Audit. There are always new online systems and tools that may make it possible to automate something you're doing manually. Ask yourself (as well as your "front line" team members), "Is there a better way to do this?"

Sidenote

There are two types of online tools out there: those built for corporations and those built for small business. In my experience the main difference is the cost – something created for big corporate business will always cost a lot more than something built for individuals or small business, even if they do the exact same thing! A good example is a Customer Relationship Management (CRM) system. Salesforce.com is a popular system that costs hundreds of dollars per month. By comparison, the Highrise system from the folks at 37 Signals is a simplified CRM system (perfect for the less complex needs of online business owners) and its price starts at $24 per month. Most corporate tools have features that the small business owner doesn't need and therefore shouldn't have to pay for.

I remember when one of our favorite online calendars went "big business." We had been spending $97 per year for a small business subscription, but when they decided to change their target market to bigger companies that need online scheduling capabilities, they started charging $99 per month! It was the same system, just a different target market that would pay more. Needless to say, we had to look for a different solution (Google Calendar is an excellent online scheduling tool, and FREE as of the time of writing). The moral of this story is that if you find an online tool that looks great but costs a lot, keep digging because chances are there is a less expensive option that can do the same thing.

It is also really important to plan for continued business growth and to act as though your client is a big company (even if they aren't yet).

If you look for systems that have varying packages and options that can grow with the business, this can save you the stress of having to switch systems down the road. As an example, in order to help one of my clients look more professional, we recently signed up for a toll-free phone number. The toll-free service provider offers lots of bells and whistles. Right now we're using the simplest option; however everything is ready to go for when my client needs to add additional extensions or other options.

Automating is one of my favorite things about working online. Anything that will take a task off my plate is ideal in my mind.

(7) BUILDING THE TEAM

. . . .

PEOPLE MANAGEMENT

*Clients want someone to help build
and manage their virtual team*

In the virtual world, most clients rely on a team of contractors to support their business, and rarely look to hire people as employees. Even though hiring is a fact of life when it comes to owning a business, I have yet to meet a small business owner who actually enjoys the process of finding, hiring and managing their team. Many business owners have gone through the process of finding and hiring (usually a VA or a web designer) and in many cases have struggled to make it work. They know they need a team to help in various areas, but they do not enjoy the process of hiring and delegating.

This is a huge area of need for most business owners, and the role of the OBM is highly important here.

Keeping it lean

As discussed in the last chapter, I'm a big fan of automating before you hire. As such, I tend towards hiring a smaller, leaner team for my clients. The core team of key people will generally consist of the business owner (your client), the OBM (you) and usually one VA or support person. Depending on the business there may also be a delivery team, such as a group of associate coaches who help the client run their programs.

Outside of this key team there will be a number of contractors that you will call on from time to time for various projects. This may include copywriters, web/blog designers, graphic designers, A/V specialists, SEO professionals, Internet marketing strategists, business coaches, etc. Part of the beauty of working online is that there are so many wonderful contractors out there who can step in on an "as needed" basis. Gone are the days when anyone has to do it all. Now a business owner can have a core team, and then turn to specialists in these various areas when the business requires it.

"The more complex anything is, the more chances there are for something small to make it go off course"

• ANDREA J. LEE

In my experience, if there are too many people on the core team it can make for a very confusing and overly busy environment. Similar to having too many cooks in the kitchen, when there are too many people on the core team they can end up stepping all over each other and nothing gets done. Plus, the more people there are on the core team, the more diluted the responsibility becomes. An ideal team has only a few people at the core who are responsible for getting stuff done and for managing the other contractors who are doing the work.

Let's use the example of a weekly core team meeting, which we highly recommend. Now I'm not a big fan of meetings for the sake of meetings (which is why I no longer work in the corporate world, heheh) but a weekly touch-base meeting for the core team is essential. Even though we rely on email for most of our day-to-day communication, nothing can take the place of a live conversation to keep the big picture alive.

As a three-way call between you (the OBM), your client (the business owner) and a VA, this meeting can be a quick and efficient way to get updates on projects, go over details of what's coming up, etc. But as you bring other people into the meeting, it starts to muddy the waters. For example, not everyone needs to know the specific tasks that the web designer is working on – it will confuse people and bring them into conversations that they have no role in. It's far better to meet weekly with the core team, who can then turn around and update peripheral team members.

As the OBM you want to work with your client to help define, source, hire, train and manage team members.

1. Defining

Defining the team is taking a look at the business needs and identifying what kind of help is needed. This is where your expertise will come in, as you need to know enough about the process of doing business online to know what kind of help you need to hire. It is VERY important to know exactly what you are hiring someone to do, so as to prevent confusion down the road on both sides.

For example, say you want to create a video for your client to put up on their homepage. Does the person you're hiring need to do everything from A-Z (identify the content, create the content, produce the video, edit it and coordinate with your web master to put it on the homepage)? Or will your client record the video with their webcam and you just need someone to add an intro and convert it into a format that you can put online? There's a big difference between those two jobs.

Once you are clear on the needs of the business you can look at putting together job descriptions for people you need to hire. Don't be intimidated by the terminology - it doesn't need to be a standard corporate 5 page job description - you just need to outline the skills, abilities and availability that you are looking for. It is also a good idea to define how much you are willing to pay as contractors rates can vary.

2. Sourcing

Once you've defined the needs, you can look for people to fill those roles. We are asked all the time how business owners can find people to join their team. We always recommend that you look first to your own network – start with who you know. If you need someone to create a video for you, simply send a note to your network asking if anyone knows a good A/V professional. 90% of the time someone will have a recommendation of someone they have used themselves or heard good things about. Likewise, they may also be able to warn you against using certain people and save you some potential headache.

Most likely, as an OBM you probably have your own core team of contractors who you've used for projects in the pasts. I have my own rolodex of specialists in various areas who I can call on to use with any of my OBM clients – I know them, trust their work and because we have an established relationship they are quite responsive to my needs and will often "bump me up the list" even if they are super busy.

If you aren't able to find someone via your network, then you will need to reach out to other sources. Elance.com and

Guru.com are great places to find contractors for all kinds of online skill sets and projects. In fact, some of our best team members came from Elance – Andrea and I hired someone to help with event management and she ended up being a key part of our team for years. Another one of our best team members came from a Craigslist.com posting just over a year ago.

Being that you aren't hiring a full-time employee, I wouldn't look towards the traditional strategies of posting a job ad in newspapers or via online job boards such as Monster.com. Not only is that an expensive option, chances are that you will not attract contractors as most people who peruse job ads are looking for full time employment.

Sidenote

The current buzz online is all about how to use social media to market your business and find new clients. Not only are social media tools great for marketing, they can also be a highly effective way to source team members.

You could post your project request on Twitter, use your "Status Update" in Facebook or send a targeted message to your LinkedIn or Ryze community. Part of what is so great about these social networks is that not only are you reaching YOUR friends, but with the six degrees of separation you're also reaching friends of friends who might be the ones to fill your needs.

3. Hiring

I've found that unless you are hiring a core team member, you don't need to do a traditional interview route with most contractors. What you do need to do is ensure that they have the skills you are looking for.

Ask to see their portfolio, and particular examples of projects similar to yours. If you are hiring someone for a big project, such as a website redesign, you may want to ask them for references where they've done similar work. Keep it simple, other online business owners won't have the time to answer a lot of reference questions for you. I would simply just ask the person how it was to work with the contractor, and if they have any tips for doing so. You may just get a few "they are great!" responses, which in my mind counts as a good reference.

Check on the contractor's availability and timelines – how long will it take them to finish your project? What is their current workload? When can they start? If they are super busy they may not be able to start for a month and you may need something in a week.

What are their rates and how do they want to be paid? We prefer to pay people via PayPal, and some international contractors don't like to use PayPal. This is something to discuss upfront as this can cause an issue later on if payment options are limited.

Once you've found a match, the hiring process is usually as simple as getting started! I generally don't worry too much about formal agreements unless we are hiring a core team member. If someone is just going to be editing an audio file for you, it seems a bit much to ask them to sign an agreement upfront. In most cases, it's enough to send an email outlining what you discussed about the project, such as the deliverables from them, the timeline for completion and the budget. Ask them to reply to the email and voilà! You have a basic agreement in place. For example, I would send an email that says:

Hi Beth,

I just wanted to follow up with an email to confirm what we talked about today.

As discussed, I am looking for a custom illustrated banner for my blog site at www.MommyVAs.com. I'm looking for the banner to be 800 pixels wide and no taller than 200 pixels. I'd like the illustration to be of me on my computer and my girls around me. I've attached a picture of us that you can use as a reference. I really like this banner at examplewebsite.com as an example. [It's really nice to include an example for them to work from where possible.]

I'm looking to have a draft by next Wednesday, and will need the final done by Friday, which you confirmed works on your end. The cost for the banner will be $100, which includes one revision and final copy, to be paid to you via PayPal on completion of banner.

Will you please let me know if I've missed anything? If this looks good, just pop me a quick note to say 'great' and we are ready to roll. Thanks!

Or, if you have being going back and forth via email to discuss the project, those emails will also suffice as an agreement. Just be sure to keep a copy of them in case you ever need to refer back to confirm rates, etc.

Before hiring a core team member I recommend trying them out on a single project or two first, to ensure that there is a fit for the role (you never really know until they get to work). When you are ready to bring them onto the team long-term, have them sign a Contractors Agreement outlining their role, responsibilities, termination notice, contractors status, etc. If you don't already have a Contractors Agreement, you'll find one in The OBM Toolbox at the back of this book.

4. Training

Depending on the role, you may need to train a person on the various systems and tools that you use. Being that you've already created an SOP (as discussed in the last chapter) this will streamline the training process as it gives new team members a place to turn to for a 'how-to' reference. It is also a great way for you to see where the gaps are in your SOP, as you will find yourself saying, "Here's how to do this ... ooops, that's not in there yet," or responding to questions that highlight what's missing. So you can update the SOP along the way.

I've found that it is still best to take a bit of time to actually walk a person through their role, responsibilities and the bigger picture of the business. If you just say, "Here's the SOP, go to work!" it generally doesn't give them enough of a foundation to work from. Take the time to schedule a phone call, give them a tour of your client's websites and backend systems and show them where to find the information they need in the SOP. If you give people the big picture it gives them something bigger to plug into, which I've found to be so important in the long run. If your team members get what is going on from a bigger perspective, they will be able to contribute in larger ways down the road.

Sidenote

Skills Not Required. Be open to the idea of hiring someone who may not yet have all the skills you need. When I worked for a local placement company in Calgary (before I worked online) we used to say, "Hire for personality, not for skills." Anyone can learn a skill, but personality and fit can not be taught.

This means, of course, that you may have to spend more time and effort in training someone. In our experience we've found that the people that we've trained from scratch almost always work out better than those we hired based on skills only. In some cases a person who comes with 'skills intact' may be already set in their way of doing things and have to unlearn it. This is way more work in the long run than just training them fresh.

There are always exceptions to the rule of course, and if you can find someone who is a great fit and already has the skills, well, that is ideal! Just don't discount someone who doesn't know your systems if you notice that they "click" well with you and the business. A little investment in training this person could pay dividends in the long run.

Me and my shadow

One of our favorite training methodologies is shadowing – have the person follow you around virtually so they can learn in "real time." This is very easy to do online, simply blind carbon copy (Bcc) the trainee on various emails that apply to what they need to learn, and follow up as needed to explain things in greater detail.

This is highly effective for a couple of reasons. First, it keeps training from becoming a new task in your already busy schedule. Instead, you can train the person within the natural flow of the business. As various situations come up, shadow them on the process and send them extra instructions or details as needed.

Secondly, people are much more likely to remember something when they see it "live and in-action" versus hear about it in theory. When you try to teach everything up front, chances are that most of the information won't stick as they haven't had a chance to apply it. Whereas when you teach via shadowing, the trainee gets to see real examples of the situations and will retain the information at a much higher level.

Don't forget to assign your trainee the task of updating the SOP along the way with the various things they are learning.

5. Managing

In our project management chapter we already talked about managing as it applies to "getting stuff done." This is where the OBM spends alot of time on a day-to-day basis.

Outside of the day-to-day stuff, I also really love to work with team members on their own growth and expansion. Apply your coaching approach and get to know them at a deeper level. What are the goals of those who are on your team? How can you help them work towards those goals and give them some experience to get there? For example, your VA may have a real interest in blog design. Perhaps they could work on creating a new template for your client's blog the next time it needs a bit of freshening up?

For me, there is nothing more rewarding than seeing a fellow team member grow into a new specialty or focus for their own business. In some cases this may mean that they stop working for you in order to focus on this new area of their business.

In my work with Andrea, we have always considered the VA role to be a place to come and grow versus to come and stay. On average, our VAs stay with us for about two years and then they move onto bigger and better things. Human beings are meant to grow and expand, in both work and in life. If you really get this and come to expect this from your team members then it doesn't have to be a bad thing when someone moves on. It becomes a graduation of sorts, something to celebrate, and chances are they can still remain a part of your team with their new focus.

In fact, Andrea likes to say that one of her definitions of success in business is how many contractors go on to become so huge she would never want to have to afford them.

The OBM is also responsible for taking care of any challenges that come up within the team. Perhaps someone is late with their projects, or keeps making mistakes, or maybe two team members are not getting along for some reason. The key here is to simply treat people with respect and have an honest conversation about it. Open a dialogue and find out what's up. Something may be going on in their personal life that is causing them stress. Or they may be getting so busy in their business that they are having a hard time keeping up.

Then, give them the chance to suggest how they would like to fix the situation; put the ball in their court. People are much more likely to stick to a solution that they created themselves than a solution that is imposed upon them. If they are simply so busy in their business that they can't keep up perhaps it is time for them to let go of some of the work they are doing for you and pass it along to someone else? This gives them the opportunity to choose the work they enjoy doing and let go of the stuff they don't like quite as much, which is something that team members earn along the way.

Understand too that everyone makes mistakes – unless you start to see a pattern of mistakes it probably isn't cause for any kind of intervention. Part of the beauty of working online is that everything is fixable. Compared to offline mistakes (e.g., putting the wrong address in a Yellow Pages ad) you can fix most online mistakes quickly and easily. If someone setup the wrong price for a product in the shopping cart, fix it and contact anyone it may apply to. If there is an error on a webpage this can be easily corrected. Or maybe a broadcast is sent out with the wrong link in it – just resend the broadcast with an apology and the correct link.

There seems to be a rite of passage in working online – what I call the First Big Mistake. Every VA that I've ever worked with has had this happen, myself included! I remember my first big mistake was when I started to work with CoachVille back in 2002. I was working on a website where Thomas Leonard had taken some beautiful pictures of coaches during one of his road trips and created an online gallery. Well, I went ahead and accidentally over-wrote the index.html on the home page of this site – and I didn't have a backup copy! I felt my heart sink, and was so upset when I told Andrea (who was GM of CoachVille at the time) what had happened. Andrea said, "Oooops, just create another page, then." And so I did – fixed!

Now the thing about the big mistake is that it makes you become much more careful with the work you do. You'd better believe I check twice before I ever upload an index.html page these days!

Stepping into an existing team

Quite often you will be joining a team that is already working with the client (and in some cases has been around a very long time). You may be familiar with some of the team members already, especially if you have done a previous project or two with the client (which we do recommend before taking on the OBM role, and we'll talk more about that later). There is a bit of an art to joining an already established team, so here are a few tips:

- Understand how the other team members are feeling. You are essentially a stranger who is coming in to play a pretty important role in the business. It is natural for people to be a bit suspicious or unsure of you until they get to know you. It is your responsibility to tread lightly in the beginning and give people an opportunity to get to know, like and trust you. Be authentic and don't try to "play a role."

The role of an OBM is quite new to them (assuming that your client hasn't had an OBM before), and they may not be used to what it is that you are doing in the business. They may be used to going directly to your client for everything, and it may take some time to create and establish new channels of communication in the team. In some cases they are quite happy to have another person to go to, as the client may have been too busy or not quite sure how to handle certain situations. Suggesting they read a copy of this book can help out too.

- Ask them to co-create with you. Your role as the OBM is to *coordinate* the growth of the business, not to *take over*. Make it very clear that you want and need their input, especially as it applies to streamlining and simplifying business systems and processes. An existing team is a goldmine of ideas for how to fix and improve things.

- Get to know them. What are their own personal goals for their business? What else would they love to try and grow into within the business? What do they do for fun outside of work? When you make a personal connection with someone it can make working together a more enjoyable experience

Building up your own delegation habit

After working with Alexandria Brown for nine years, Liz Murphy has made the transition from being Ali's VA to being her Business and Operations Manager. Liz now manages a team of nine people for a multi-million dollar business. There have cer-

141

tainly been challenges along the way, however the biggest challenge for Liz has been breaking the habit of "doing" versus "managing."

*As Liz says "My job is to manage the team to ensure that things get done, I'm no longer the one who is doing the work. This has been a tough habit for me to break, as I've always been a doer. Ali has challenged me to **not do anything** – instead I need to make sure that team members are trained and equipped to do all the tasks assigned. At times it may seem easier for me to just do something versus training someone how to do it. When that happens, I remind myself that the investment of training may be more work in the moment, however in the long run it pays for itself over and over again."*

I can so relate to what Liz is saying, and in fact I fall victim to this much more that I care to admit! Any good OBM has been the one doing the work at some point – this is the best way to learn and get the experience we need to play the OBM role. So our natural inclination is to do the work ourselves, usually without giving it a second thought.

However as your client's business grows (which it surely will, with your help), it is simply impossible for you to be both doer and manager. Even if it doesn't seem necessary right now, I invite you to start working on your delegation muscle. And let your clients know, so they can be paying you to do what you do best – manage. You'll hire others, at a lesser rate, for the "doing."

8 LOOKING AT THE NUMBERS

....

MONEY MANAGEMENT

Clients want someone who can help them look at the bottom line

I remember one of my professors in my last semester of college asking us, "What is the definition of a business?"

Being students, we came up with some pretty lengthy and in-depth descriptions. The answer itself was surprisingly simple.

A business makes money.

If you aren't making money (or working towards making money) than you don't have a business, you have a hobby.

(And it's truly surprising how many businesses are really hobbies, but that is a whole other topic.)

I always find it funny that business owners want to make money, but many of them seem almost allergic to managing their money. They may be very good at bringing in revenue, and may in fact have a consistent six- or seven-figure income. But ask them any specifics about their revenue or expenses and they just shake their heads and assume that since money is coming in they must be doing OK. Outside of getting a yearly income statement from their accountant, many business owners don't keep proper track of what is going on with their money on a regular basis.

Is their business really making money? Is their income larger than their expenses? You hear about people who win millions in the lottery and end up penniless within years. Well, sadly there are a surprising number of businesses that can tell a similar story – they may have really high revenues but actually not have money in the bank at the end of the day.

Making money is not the name of the game – profit is the name of the game. In order to earn a profit, you need to make more than you spend. So if you want to make more money, there are only two ways to do it: increase your income or decrease your expenses.

It is vital for any business to keep track of their numbers on a regular basis in order to know if they're making a profit. I'm not talking about being an accountant here, what I'm talking about is common sense money management. And as an OBM, you can help by collecting the information the client needs in order to truly see what is going on in their business. With this information in hand they can measure their success (or lack thereof) in various areas of their business, make changes, try new things and see how those changes affect the numbers that count.

So what should you track? Let's break it down a bit

Web statistics

Being an online-based business, your client's website is usually the hub of their business activity, and traffic plus conversion is the magic formula of growing a business online. So track how many people are visiting your client's websites, and of those visitors how many are taking action (e.g., signing up for a freebie or making a purchase).

With this information you can see exactly where your client's business can be improved. If they have decent traffic but aren't making any sales, you need to focus on conversion. If there isn't much traffic coming to the websites, look at ways to boost traffic. As you continually work towards improving your clients' websites (as you should), you will be able to see improvement in the numbers, as well.

A good web statistics program such as Google Analytics will give you all the information you need. As of the time of writing Google Analytics is free; sign up for an account at: www.google.com/analytics/. This is something I would track on a monthly basis (or weekly if your client has a lot of traffic, say 1,000 visitors or more in a day).

The list

In the online world your client's list is King. Every online business should have a list of targeted (interested) people with whom they keep in touch on a regular basis. This is a very important part of relationship-based selling and long-term sustainability. They may have sub-divided lists such as prospects (usually called an ezine or newsletter list), clients, affiliates and perhaps potential clients.

You want to keep track of the number of people on your client's various lists. Also, track how many people join each week and each month. When you see a surge in subscriptions, what caused it? How can you replicate that again?

For example, we recently saw a surge of signups to one of Andrea lists, and with a bit of digging we found out that a JV partner had recently done a big promotion for their own product and we were getting exposure on their Thank You page. That led us to look for similar people we could swap Thank You page messages with.

Sales/Revenue

List each product, service and offering that your client sells, and anything else that brings money into the business. Then keep track of the amounts sold for each item on a weekly or monthly basis.

What is selling or not selling? Of those items that are selling, how can you continue to improve sales? Of those that aren't selling, how can you increase sales or perhaps look at letting that item go? (Just because something is for sale doesn't mean you have to sell it forever.)

Promotions

Whenever you do a promotion you want to track the results. Ad-tracking links are great for this – you can set up a tracking link via the shopping cart system and monitor the number of clicks and sales from that specific promotion. You'll know if you've made a profit if the resulting sales are more than the cost of implementing the promotion. Keep in mind here that your costs can be both direct (such as the cost of placing an ad in someone's newsletter) or indirect (such as paying someone to manage your affiliate program in the shopping cart).

If the promotion isn't making money you can either a) revise your approach and try again or b) scrap it all together and focus on other promotional strategies. I like to use the "three strikes and you're out" rule here as well – if you try something three times and it doesn't create a profit, move on. There are lots of promotional opportunities out there, so don't get attached to something if it isn't making you money. Likewise, just because something works for someone else, that doesn't necessarily mean it will work for your client. Every business is different and will have its own best way to market and promote.

Expenses

How much money is the business spending on systems, tools and team members each month? I find this to be a particularly common area for improvement in a client's business. Chances are, your client may not have a clue about their total expenses and may be surprised (and possibly frightened) by the number.

What are the current expenses and where or how can you cut back on those expenses? I tend to err on the side of being miserly (dare I say cheap?) when it comes to systems. Why spend hundreds of dollars a month on a system that is either a) not being used or b) could be combined into another system? For example, if your client has a separate autoresponder system, affiliate system, ad tracking system and shopping cart, suggest they combine it all into an all-in-one shopping cart. The average cost of an online tool is $30 - $50/month, and you don't want your client to be paying for more of them than they need – they can really add up!

Also, how much is your client spending on team members each month? Is it necessary to have everyone on the payroll each and every month? Is each team member "paying their way" in terms of how much their work is contributing to the bottom line? Is your client paying a higher rate than necessary for certain things? Are they paying a specialist to do something that their VA could do for less? I see this happen a lot, e.g., paying a webmaster $75 per hour to send an email broadcast instead of assigning that task to the VA for $35 per hour.

In an information-based business, you generally **don't want your expenses to be more than a third of your total revenue.** If expenses are more than this then your client may need to take a good look at how they are doing business and where their money is being spent. We've found that with a few tweaks, a business owner can usually make a pretty substantial decrease to expenses to increase their profits overall.

And if you can help them do that, you better believe they will be singing praises to their OBM!

Talking dollars and sense

Even though a lot of business owners may not be 100% aware of their numbers, if you speak to them in terms of dollars they will certainly sit up and take notice.

So anytime your client is considering a new idea or strategy, be sure to "bring it home" as far as how it will affect the bottom line. For example, say your client is launching a new membership program and needs to setup a system to manage the back-end. They come to you and say, "Hey, Bob is using this great system called MemberGate – let's use that one for our new membership."

You look into it and realize that MemberGate costs $3,995 or more depending on your needs (which is quite costly, in my opinion)! As the OBM we always want to see if there is a better solution out there, so we do a bit of research and see what other business owners are using for their memberships. In talking to a few of our colleagues we discover that many of them are using aMember.com, which only costs $199. Combined with a customized blog as the "member resource area," your total costs in setting up this solution would probably be less than $1,000.

That's a potential savings of $3,000 for your client.

Now, keep in mind that when you approach your client with

these different options, you need to be able to adequately compare the two systems beyond just the initial cost difference. For example, not only is aMember less expensive, but you can customize it, while with MemberGate you are stuck using their templates. Also, with aMember you can grow to an unlimited number of members for the same low price, whereas with MemberGate once you reach 1,000 members you will need to spend another $2,500 to upgrade to the next level.

To just say to your client "aMember looks like a great solution and it's cheaper, maybe we should go with that one," isn't enough. If you approach it in a slightly different way it can have a much bigger impact. I would say to my client "Here are the two options, which have a difference of $3,000 in upfront costs. Based on your membership model of charging $27 per month per member, with MemberGate you won't see a profit until after 150 subscriptions, whereas with the aMember system you will be able to enjoy a profit after just 37 subscriptions."

Because it's not just about the cost – it's about overall profit and how quickly they can reach that point. When you bring it back to that bottom line for your clients they will be able to make the best decision possible and enjoy more profits with less effort.

As a side benefit, you are also training your clients to start to think about profit in their business. Again, many business owners tend to look at revenue only and really aren't giving profit the proper consideration. You're helping them to connect the dots – they come to understand that, "When I do X, it means Y to my bottom line." This additional benefit to having an OBM on the team can really help a business owner start to focus their energy and attention where it counts – the balance in their bank account at the end of the day.

LIVING THE DREAM

MAKING MORE WHILE WORKING LESS

You know you want to!

The standard business model of a service-based professional is the exchange of time for money. You work a certain amount of time, and you are paid an hourly wage for that time. Almost everyone I've talked to in the industry works this way, including the many OBMs that I interviewed while writing this book. The thing is that there are only so many hours in a day, and only a certain number of those that you are able to work.

Say that you have decided that you have 20 hours a week

available to work in and on your business, in order to keep the balance of your time for your family as well as time for yourself.

Of those 20 hours, it's likely that 15 are billable hours – you'll need the rest of the time for administrative and marketing activities.

If you are charging your clients $35 per hour as a virtual assistant and you are working 15 billable hours a week, that equals $525 per week or $2,100 per month. If you plan on taking off four weeks of vacation per year, this works out to be $25,200 of revenue from your business for the year.

$25,000 a year is a good income for working part-time hours and enjoying the flexibility that a virtually based business allows, however that is the limit that you can make under this model of exchanging time for money. If you want to work a maximum of 20 hours a week at $35 per hour you will make $25K and no more.

What if you want to make more money in your business?

How would you like to make $40,000 a year? At $35 per hour that would require that you work about 28 hours a week (given that 5-ish hours a week are non-billable). You could certainly work these extra hours, however I'm guessing that you started your home-based business for a reason and that adding more hours that would take you away from your family may not be feasible for you.

The time-for-money model puts a limit on the success of your business – not only from a monetary perspective, but also from a satisfaction and growth perspective.

How can I make more money while working the same (or less) hours?

Would you like to be able to have unlimited growth opportunity in your online support business, even if you are already at the bursting point? What if you could make more money while working the same or less hours? If this sounds attractive to you, then read on!

There are a few options that will allow you the freedom to increase your income without adding to your workload.

Option 1: Raise your hourly rates

There are two ways to increase your rates and making more money per hour: you can start charging more for the "regular" VA work that you do, or you can start doing "specialty" work that you can charge a higher rate for.

Regular VA skills

These are the foundational skills that business owners are looking for in a virtual assistant, and for which you would charge your regular rates.

- Shopping cart administration
- Merchant accounts
- Ezine broadcasting
- Basic website maintenance / FTP
- Autoresponder Setup
- Blog posting
- Article submission
- Affiliate administration
- Customer service
- Online audio recording
- Word processing / Typing
- Email management
- Creating PDF documents
- Online research
- PowerPoint presentations
- Database management

Specialty skills

These are specialty skills that most clients need on a project basis, and for which you will want to charge your higher rates.

- Website design
- Graphic design
- Writing / Editing
- Transcription
- Copywriting
- Audio / Video editing
- Blog Design / customization
- Bookkeeping
- Event management
- Project management
- Internet marketing strategy
- Search engine marketing (including Google Adwords)
- Joint venture sourcing and management
- Online business management

At the time of writing, the industry standard for regular VA services is in the $25-$45 per hour range. How do you know where to set your rates within that range? It depends on both your experience and your clientele. Generally, VAs charge on the lesser end if they are just getting started or are still developing the full set of skills that they would like to offer. Once you have more experience you can raise your hourly rate accordingly.

Clients in certain industries may pay less than others, so get to know what the standard rates are for the clients you are working with. Having worked with coaches and consultants over the years, I've found that most of them are looking to pay in the $25-$35 per hour range, and they really don't want to pay more than that if they can help it. Keep in mind that if most people are charging say $20 per hour to serve your target market and you suddenly raise your rates to $40 per hour this may affect how often you are hired in comparison to your fellow VAs.

And do be considerate of raising your rates with current clients. I'm a huge fan of giving your current clients a special VIP rate as thanks for their long term business. Of course they will appreciate this as well, so if you do raise your rates be sure to let them know they are getting a VIP rate.

You may be thinking, "Hey, I know my skills are worth more than the standard rates," and you would like to charge a higher hourly rate. Be prepared to answer the question:

Why should I pay you $50 an hour when I can hire your fellow VA for $30 an hour?

If you are offering a specialized service of any kind this will certainly justify a higher hourly rate (usually in the $50-$100 per hour range). A specialized service is something that requires a level of special training, such as web design or graphic design.

Of course being an OBM falls into the range of specialty skills, as you are providing a higher level of service to your clients.

I was talking to Amy Taggart of DesignFormare.com about raising rates. Amy has been working as a VA for just over a year now, in conjunction with the web and graphic design business that she's had for 10 years. She has been at the 'bursting point' in her business for months now, and has decided that she really needs to shift her focus to some higher paying work. Her lower-paying VA work has her so busy these days that she's had to say no to some higher-paying design projects that have come across her plate. In her own words:

"I can work 15 hours a day at my VA rate or work 8 hours a day at my design rate, and still make the same amount of money. It's time for me to make some changes."

Charging a higher rate for specialized services is a great example of how to escape the bursting zone without losing any income.

Option #2: Hire your own team

Hire other VAs and support professionals to work as part of your team, so you can take on more business and not have to do all the work yourself. More and more virtual assistants are taking this route once they hit the bursting point. Rather than turn away clients, they hire their own team of VAs and create a multi-VA business.

The plus side of this option is that it allows a VA to truly become a scalable, growth-oriented business. The have the option to grow their business (and income) as much as they want, depending on how many people they have on their team. You can continue to charge what you've been charging, and pay a percentage of that rate to the VAs on your team.

A few considerations if you decide to go this route:

• As you grow your team your role becomes less of a 'doer' and more of a manager of everything that is going on – you essentially become your own OBM! Some people find this to be a bit of a challenge, especially if they enjoy being a VA and working directly with clients.

• You are responsible for the work that your team members are doing, and as such you need to set up systems and training to ensure they are delivering quality work. This requires working quite closely with team members, more closely than you may think. It's easy to assume that people will provide the same level of service and do things the way you would, whereas in reality they may need a lot of training and coaching to do so (especially at the beginning). Stay plugged into your team members and what they are doing.

- There are no guarantees with people – someone on your team may have to quit suddenly for whatever reason, which could leave you scrambling to complete the work that they are responsible for. I've seen it happen time and again, both in my previous life as a corporate recruiter and as an online business manager. You think you have the perfect team than BAM! Someone quits or makes a big mistake and you are left with a mess to fix. Just know that this will happen at some point. It's not a matter of IF it's a matter of WHEN. The key is to be prepared and calm in the moment, and to look for immediate solutions and replacements so that your clients still receive the level of service they require.

- Some clients may really want to work with you directly, and may not want to work with other members of your team. This is especially common when you started with them as a "team of one" and then began growing your business along the way. On the flip side, other clients really like the fact that they are hiring a team so that they have more than one person to rely on.

- You need to have very strong time tracking and project management systems in place with a team. Who is working on what for which clients? You need to be able to answer that question at a glance. Plus you are responsible for billing for all the work done each month, which in itself can become a huge task.

If you are going to build your own VA team you will essentially become a business in your own right – complete with all the challenges (headaches!) and rewards (money!) of owning a growth-based business. I very consciously made a decision a number of years ago that I didn't want to go this route. I am aware of how much work it can be (compared to a solo practice) and with family commitments I'm not willing or able to go there. It comes down to personal choice, knowing the differences between working solo versus creating your own team.

As an OBM, you can work with your own team or as a solo. I know a few OBMs who bring a team with them, providing the "full meal deal" service for their clients. Other OBMs (such as myself) work with a client's existing team members and/or hire other team members to work direct with the client.

From a day-to-day perspective the work you are doing with the team will look the same – you are responsible for managing the team members, ensuring that things get done in a timely manner with a focus on generating revenue. My preference to work solo is ideal for the client who doesn't want to have all their eggs in one basket. I'm a big fan of "spreading the risk" for business owners. If everyone who works with them is part of a single company, what happens if that company can no longer work with that business owner (they quit, have a falling out with the owner, etc.)?

This leaves the business owner without ANYONE on their team, which in my mind is a very scary situation. Compare that to having a number of independent contractors that work directly for the client; as team members come and go (which they always will), the business owner still has other members of the team to fill in and keep things afloat while replacements are found.

Again, it comes down to the business owner's preference. Some people really like having that "full meal deal" solution, and don't mind having the risk of all eggs in one basket. Whereas other business owners are fine with (and may prefer) having a team of independent contractors supporting their business.

Option #3: Working on incentive

I am such a HUGE fan of this option, and am surprised that of all the VAs, OBMs and other online specialists I've been interviewing these past few months, only one person is doing any kind of incentive-based payment structure.

Incentive-based pay means that you get paid a percentage of the revenue or profit that your clients make, be it on individual projects or in their business income as a whole.

This is the icing on the cake when it comes to working as an OBM, and in my humble opinion it should be the goal of any OBM-client relationship for a few reasons:

- The sky is the limit when it comes to potential earnings – as your client's business grows (as it will, with your help) your income will grow alongside.

- You are truly invested in the success of your clients business because the more they make the more you make. When you are paid hourly, you will make the same amount of money regardless of how well your client's business is doing. This is not to say that you don't care about your client's success if you are working hourly – it is important regardless– but being paid on incentive brings it to a whole new level.

- There is a much higher level of satisfaction in this working arrangement, knowing that you will benefit alongside your client as you help them grow their business. Being that an OBM plays such an important role in a business, it is only fair that they are rewarded as such. It can be a tough pill to swallow (even on a subconscious level) to see your client's business grow by leaps and bounds and still get paid the same amount as you were at the beginning. Even raising your hourly rates still leaves your income capped.

The heart of the OBM-client partnership is in sharing the growth of the business, both energetically and financially. This is what every OBM should be working towards with their clients, as it really is the full expression of a successful partnership on both sides. The client has someone that is truly plugged into the success of their business (which is what every business owner wants) and the OBM is being rewarded for their commitment in a bigger way. Now that's a recipe for a long-term successful partnership!

What does an incentive-based pay structure look like?

As an OBM you need to be paid some kind of base retainer or "draw against commission" amount plus a percentage-based incentive.

BASE + INCENTIVE = OBM INCOME

I generally recommend that you choose a flat rate for a span of hours as your base pay. For example, you could have a flat rate of $1,000/month which covers working 20-ish hours in a month. You can loosely base this amount on your hourly rate multiplied by the expected number of hours you will work in a month. Some months you may work a bit more than the 20-ish hour range, other months it may be less. In my experience this all evens out in the end (and is irrelevant anyhow as you are really being paid on incentive).

Sidenote

There is no such thing as working on commission only. There are lot of business owners out there who think that incentive-based payment should mean that there is no base and you get paid strictly on commission only. It makes sense in theory, but in reality it simply doesn't work.

As I've explained to business owners many times, in order for someone to be willing to invest time and energy in their company they need to know that they are being paid something, at least a base payment of some kind. It takes a while for incentive-based payment to really kick in, which means that someone could be expected to work for free before they ever make a dime. Like anyone else, VAs and OBMs need to make a living, and will go where the money is. Even if there is the potential to make oodles of money down the road, they need to pay bills now.

Besides, most business owners who want someone to work commission only are asking for that because they aren't making money yet in their business and can't afford to pay someone. If that is the case, they aren't ready to hire an OBM yet anyways (or anyone for that matter). A business owner who is ready for and understands the importance of hiring an OBM will gladly pay a base as part of your incentive package.

The incentive comes from an agreed upon percentage of revenue from either a) one or more business lines or b) their business income as a whole. This can vary depending on how you are working with the client. You may be paid a percentage of their programs, events and product sales, because those are the areas where you're providing support, but nothing from their individual coaching income, because you're not involved in that aspect of the business. It all depends on how your work is affecting the bottom line.

The incentive also kicks in when you help a client reach a certain revenue milestone. For example, before you came along your client was making $10K a month from their membership program. Being that an OBM's job is to help the client grow their business, your incentive based pay could kick in when their revenue hits $15K a month, something they couldn't have done without your help. Makes sense, right?

Percentage-wise you are generally looking at anywhere from 10%-25% of revenue, again depending on what the client is doing. This needs to be based on the client's business model and associated expenses. For example, they may run a monthly coaching program and also need to pay their associate coaches a percentage of the revenue. In that case, you may be looking at the 10% range. However, they may also be selling a number of information products (books, CD sets, etc.) that have less overhead costs, and therefore your share could be in the 20 - 25% range. You could have a mix of incentives for each different revenue stream with the same client.

I also highly recommend that the incentive be based on revenue and not profit.

To base payment on profit is simply a headache – in order to figure out what you are paid each month you will need to wait for all expenses to come in, allocate them to each revenue stream and then determine what you should be paid. Then there is always the complication of expenses that could be applied equally to one or more revenue streams – it can quickly get very complicated!

If you are paid on revenue it is a straightforward calculation – we made $X in sales this month so I get 10%, done!

In my experience it is cleaner and simpler to base incentive off revenue versus profit. Some clients may not want to go that route, in which case it is fine to base it on profit. Just note that the percentage amounts will need to be higher.

Breaking the hourly habit

Some people are scared of incentive-based pay. Why? It means that you have to think about your income in a totally different way.

Instead of knowing that you will be paid $X for the time work each month, you are taking the risk that your income could fluctuate. You could end up working a whole bunch of hours just to get a base amount each month! If you'd worked the same amount of hours for an hourly rate you would be paid more.

Breaking the hourly habit is about accepting the uncertainty of incentive-based pay. Yes, there is the risk of working more hours than you're paid for. The flip side, of course, is that you could also end up making more (MUCH more, in the long run) than you would hourly.

There is no guarantee either way, which is part of the risk, and I know some VAs who simply aren't willing to go that route. They prefer the assurance of knowing that if they work 20 hours this month that is what they'll be paid for. There's nothing wrong with this, it just comes down to personal choice based on your tolerance for risk.

Working on incentive also requires that you step it up and play a bigger game. You are taking on a level of responsibility that simply is not there with an hourly payment structure. Being paid on incentive puts you in the spotlight, so that if revenue targets aren't achieved you have to answer to that. This can be quite intimidating for some, although I'm a big fan of stepping into the fear and going for it anyways. It really gives you an opportunity to stretch in ways you may not have considered before, and to enjoy the ride of seeing a business grow, stumble and thrive (one of the best rides out there!).

Personally, I hate getting paid on an hourly basis; partially because I hate having to "punch a clock" (flashback to my corporate days!) but mostly because I don't think the value of my service comes from how much time I spend doing something. It comes from how what I'm doing is going to affect the client's business. If I spend five hours setting up an online customer help desk (such as Kayako.com), which in turn saves my clients countless hours of admin time in responses along with lost revenue due to missed emails, what is that really worth? Is it worth five hours at my hourly rate? Or is it worth what it saves my client on the bottom line?

10 THE GOOD, THE BAD AND THE (NOT SO) UGLY

REAL LIFE AS AN OBM

Know Thyself

Before you dive into becoming an OBM for your current or future clients, I'd like to take a moment for you to review all the benefits and pitfalls of working at this level.

Having worked as an OBM for over 5 years now, I'm rather partial to playing this bigger role for clients. However, I also know some people who have dipped their toe in the water of working as an OBM (and in some cases jumped right into the pool) only to find that it wasn't for them. This resulted in some big stress and broken relationships as the OBMs weren't able to deliver what they promised to their clients.

So I invite you to take a good, honest look at yourself in the mirror here, and I daresay that by the end of the chapter you will either feel a) excited about becoming an OBM or b) really not inspired at all by the idea. (Remember, fear can be a good thing, so if you are afraid that could be a sign that you are ready to shift into this bigger role!)

Why it's great to be an OBM

Significant earning potential

As we discussed in the last chapter, working as an OBM offers the opportunity to make significantly more money than you would in a traditional VA or online support role. Getting out of the mindset of being paid money in exchange for time and shifting to an incentive-based pay system literally blows the roof off of any income limitations.

By way of example, with one of my clients I was working on average about 25 hours a month (some months less, some months a bit more). She offered a series of 6-month coaching programs which became very popular in her niche market. As a result, I was making anywhere from $2,000-$5,000 a month as part of my incentive plan. That works out to be over $100 per hour for the 25-ish hours I was working in a month – well worth my effort, yes? Imagine having two or three clients that you work with at this level – that could be a very lucrative living for working part-time from the comfort of home.

Of course this didn't happen overnight; we had worked together for a couple of years before her business reached this level of income. Just know that it is absolutely possible when you work with the right client (which we'll talk about in the next chapter).

Work with a select few clients

Working as an OBM allows you to work more closely with fewer clients (generally two or three), compared to the traditional VA model of having lots of clients with varying needs and time commitments.

I love to use this analogy when it comes to client load: imagine that you are literally carrying around each client on your back. It doesn't matter if you do one hour a month for them or 40 hours a month, they each weigh the same amount. This can get pretty heavy if you have a lot of clients!! And darn tiring, as well. .

Energetically there is a truth to this scenario. You are "carrying around" each client that you are engaged with. This is a huge cause of the bursting point that we talked about earlier, as an hourly based model (which we are getting away from yes?) requires that we fill those hours with work in order to make a living. And for most online support professionals this means having a lot of clients, quite often 10 or more, each of whom has different needs and deadlines.

I'm sure you've had those days when it seems like every client you have pops up demanding your services – very stressful! It can literally be a brain scrambler trying to keep track of what needs to be done for each client, not to mention how you will find the time to do all that work.

When playing a bigger role with your client in an OBM capacity, you have less people to "carry around" on your back. You have two or three clients at the most who may pop up all at once asking for help, instead of eight or ten. It's easier to focus your energy on each person, instead of feeling scattered and drained trying to keep track of it all.

Establishing yourself as an expert

When you help your clients create success, you will become considered an expert yourself in your client's niche market. When good things are happening the word gets around, and people will soon come to recognize you for the role you are playing in that success. And any good client will, of course, be gladly sharing how hiring an OBM has made all the difference for them and their business.

This kind of credibility can really open up new doors for you, bringing you different opportunities that you may never have considered before. You may be approached to do consulting or coaching with business owners to help them strategize and plan for growth, or to help train their team members on various systems and strategies. Any of these options will pay a nice hourly rate and don't have to take too much time in an already busy schedule.

Finding new clients by word of mouth

I've never had to market my OBM business at all, because every single client I've worked with has come to me by word of mouth. A business owner's dream, yes? This is the reality of working at this level – more and more business owners are eager to hire an OBM, yet so few people are officially working in this role (yet!).

When you have helped grow your client's business, word gets around and other business owners will come knocking at your door. The world of online business is a very connected community, and once people learn what you can do for your client's you will find that most (if not all) of your business will come by referral. No more marketing for you! (Just for your clients)

OBM clients are long(er) term clients

Being that you play a bigger role in your client's business, chances are that you will work with your OBM clients for a very long time. In our experience, most VAs have a core group of clients that they stay with long term (maybe 25%-50% of their hours) and outside of that they have a number of clients who come and go for various reasons. This means that they are constantly having to market themselves (which takes some effort) not to mention they have that energetic "hump" of starting to work with a new client. It takes time to get to know a new client before you really settle into a good working relationship.

That's not to say that OBM clients don't come and go. There are situations where they have to make changes to their business and that can affect your role. I once had a client who had to move back to the UK, which of course affected the US-based coaching programs that he was running. Needless to say he had to focus his efforts on his new location, which resulted in an end to our working relationship. On the flipside, I've been working with one of my clients for over four years now, and I don't foresee any end to that relationship.

You can really plug in to your client's business

There is a certain level of satisfaction that comes from working very closely with a client as their OBM. You get to celebrate the successes hand-in-hand with your clients, instead of just cheering them from the sidelines. You get to see your ideas and efforts come to life, and enjoy the results of such.

This is my favorite way to work with clients. I really love getting to know their business, getting to know them and creating something bigger together than could ever be done alone. Isn't that the whole point of business? (Or life for that matter?)

Continuous learning and growth

I remember back in my corporate recruiting days when I was interviewing people on a daily basis who were looking for new jobs. Why were they looking for something new? Nine times out of ten it was simply because they were bored. They had learned everything they could learn in their current position, and they weren't seeing any opportunity for growth with their current employer. I believe that humans are meant to constantly evolve and change, and if they aren't challenged by new opportunities or situations in their work they will become dissatisfied very quickly.

This is what is so beautiful about working as an OBM – there is ALWAYS something new to learn, something to try that you haven't tried before. Bigger ways to stretch yourself, perhaps ways you didn't even consider to be possible in the past. I find that working for online-based businesses provides an extra level of learning compared to offline businesses. The Internet literally moves at the speed of light, new online systems, tools and strategies being created every day (every minute?) that can help grow your client's business. One can get seriously stuffed at this online business buffet!

Challenges of working as an OBM

There are aspects of this role that may provide a lot of stress for the OBM. It's really a matter of being prepared and knowing what you are getting into so that you are able to handle situations and not let them get the best of you.

It's a pretty new thing

The role of an Online Business Manager is quite new in the world of business. There are no generally accepted OBM principles out there (yet!) and so each person comes to the role with a different set of expectations.

What you offer as an OBM could be very different from how a business owner defines the role. This mismatch in expectations can cause issues and stress in the early days of working together.

There are also specific challenges for management profes-sionals from the "offline" world who try to tackle the OBM role head-on only to find out that although the heart of the role is the same (grow the business!), the day-to-day reality and required expertise is quite different. If you want to be an OBM you need to know how to grow a business online.

When interviewing Online Business Managers for this book I found it quite interesting that everyone works differently. We are all playing bigger roles with our clients, but there were subtle differences in how we define the role and the type of work we do for our clients.

This is all just a reflection of the OBM role being quite new. Part of what I want to accomplish with this book is to provide you with a clear definition of the OBM role, so that you can set proper and achievable expectations with your clients from the start.

Shouldering the responsibility

When working as an OBM you are taking on a higher level of responsibility than you would be in a traditional VA or online support role. This may be more than you are used to, and for some people can feel quite uncomfortable. As an OBM your responsibility increases in a few key ways:

- You are now responsible for helping to build a business, not just for getting stuff done.
- You are no longer responsible for only what you do (which you can easily control), you are now responsible

for what others are doing and ensuring that it gets done (not always so easy to control!).

- Your client is looking for you to help increase their bottom line, which needs to be considered in everything that you are doing.

This responsibility means that if something doesn't get done or doesn't provide an intended result, you have to answer to that. You need to be willing to look at a situation, acknowledge what went wrong, your role in that and how it can be fixed. This isn't a negative thing per se, rather it is a challenge that provides an opportunity for growth (usually for all concerned, not just you as OBM).

You need to know that this WILL happen; there will be times that things don't turn out the way that was planned. There will be times that the "you know what" hits the fan for whatever reason: targets may not be reached, contractors may suddenly go MIA in the middle of a project or websites may go down in the middle of a promotion. These things will happen, so the name of the game is not to prevent them from happening, but handling them when they happen.

Business is a journey of course correction and continuation. There is no set path of success and each business has its own journey to get to their goals. It's a matter of trying something, seeing how it works, making improvements to the process and continuing on. It is a matter of being willing to look objectively at what happened and how to fix it or do it differently next time around. There are times when emotions will flare, be it yours, the client's or other members of the team. As the OBM you want to be the calm in the center of the storm, working to diffuse any emotions and get everyone moving forward.

No room for mediocrity

At this level of responsibility you will continually be challenged, and you need to be willing to stretch yourself beyond what you are used to. This is a scary process for anyone – going somewhere new and different. The key is being willing to walk into that fear and not turn away from it. The key to getting over any fear is to simply face it. We've all had these experiences in our personal lives, and the same thing applies to business.

You simply cannot be mediocre when playing this bigger role with your clients. You need to be willing to step up and become more than who you were before. Working as an OBM is, in many ways, a journey of personal and professional growth. It is an excellent opportunity to exercise business muscles that you may not have used yet, knowing that you may be sore at first but that you will soon become much stronger for it.

Sometimes people aren't prepared to stretch, and it catches

them off guard. I call this a "deer in the headlights" moment. I remember a time when I was at a recruitment training session and the facilitator called on me to role play a recruiting situation. I was caught totally off guard (I think I was daydreaming, to be honest) and my mind went blank – I couldn't think of a single thing to say! I literally sat there in silence, wishing the floor would open up and swallow me whole. It was one of the most embarrassing moments in my working life.

The thing is that I wasn't prepared for or expecting to be stretched that day. I was ready to zone out for another boring training session. So when I was asked to do a role play that was something new and uncomfortable for me, I froze. Not to say that this would never happen to me again (we all have our moments!) but I am now much more engaged in myself and willing to step it up when called upon by events or people in my life.

The risk of incentive-based payment

As already discussed, for some people the idea of incentive-based payment is quite frightening; the idea that they may work X hours and not make their hourly rate from that is a huge turnoff for them. They really want to know that they will work X and make X from that time spent.

If the idea of incentive-based payment is not an inspiration to you, then I would ask if you are really ready to become an OBM. Being paid on incentive becomes a reflection of how well you are doing your job as an OBM. If you meet your goals you will be paid more than your base. If you don't meet your goals you won't be paid more, which means that something is off and needs to be looked at.

I remember trying to put one of our VAs on an incentive-based structure at one point, where she would start to play a bigger role in some project (not an official OBM role, more like a "road to OBM" role) and get paid when we reached certain targets. She was willing to try, but then each month she would question the fact that she had worked X hours but only got paid a base which worked out to be less than her hourly rate. We discussed how this could be a temporary thing and that over time and with her continued engagement in the project there would come a tipping point where the incentive kicks in and she is being paid more than what her hourly rate would have been. For whatever reason, she didn't like this and we ended up going back to paying her hourly. There is nothing wrong with this choice at all, it simply says to me that she wasn't ready or willing to work as an OBM and was better suited to working at the VA level.

Some people simply aren't ready or willing to take on the challenge of being an OBM. They aren't willing to up the ante and have the effectiveness of their work be reflected in their income. An OBM should be excited by the prospect of incentive-based pay, as it is the heart of what their job is – making more money for their clients and subsequently for themselves.

Having your eggs in fewer baskets

As already discussed, working as an OBM means working with fewer clients at a time – usually two or three clients. So what happens if one of these clients goes away for some reason? They could have an unexpected change that comes up (such as the client who moved away) or you may decide to stop working with your client for some reason. Instead of losing maybe 10% of your income as would happen if you have 10 clients, you have now lost 30% of your income. Yipes!

This is certainly a concern for many people as they transition from VA to OBM. There is a certain safety buffer when you have lots of clients versus a few, and you need to be willing to take that leap and know that it will be fine. If you stop working with a certain client, there are many more business owners who are eager and ready to hire an OBM. Chances are you've probably had a number knock on your door already and can simply reach out to them.

Every OBM that I've talked to is now making more in their business with fewer clients, compared to when they were working as a VA. That's not to say there is a guarantee, just know that it is very common.

When life gets in the way

Take a good look at your life and ask yourself, "Do I have the time and energy to play a bigger game with my clients right now?" There may be some times in your life when you don't have the time and energy available to be an OBM for your clients.

I am the prime example here. I have two young girls, one 2.5 years old and the other 6 months old, who are both home with me most of the day. So I have made a very conscious decision that I have only 10-ish hours in a week to dedicate to my clients. My daytime hours are limited, and I've decided that I don't want to work at night, in order to keep my life sane and balanced.

As of the time of writing this book I am working with two OBM clients on a very part-time basis (up to 20 hours per month each). I actually chose to discontinue working with a client after my second daughter was born – she has a very busy business and I knew I wasn't going to be able to dedicate the time needed to play this bigger role in her business. We both discussed it and agreed that it would be better for all concerned if she found someone else.

If I was to try to take on more or busier clients it would not be fair to them (as I wouldn't be able to be as available as they would need) nor to me and my family (as I would be super-stressed and grumpy). So I have set something up that works for me and my clients. As Cindy, who is also a mother of two young children, likes to say, "I don't have the time or energy to build an empire right now." Perhaps down the road when the kids are a bit older.

So take a snapshot of your life right now and ask if you have the time and energy necessary to support your clients in this bigger way. Perhaps you have young children, or even teenage children that need more of your attention. I also know of people who have had to put their businesses on hold to take care of an ailing parent. Or maybe you have just come out of a stressful time in your life and need to keep things simple and stress-free for a while – that's fine, give yourself a break!

When it comes to the reality of working as an OBM, the rule of thumb is to "know thyself." Be very upfront and honest with who you are, what you are willing to do (and not do) and decide from there. If the role of an OBM doesn't fit right now, put it aside and come back to it in a year or two. There is no expiry date here, if anything the demand for OBMs will continue to grow exponentially as more clients realize the value of having one on their team.

⑪ MAKING THE MATCH

. . . .

YOUR IDEAL OBM CLIENT

Not all business owners are ready to hire an OBM (even if they think they are)

We've spent this whole book talking about you – the OBM. There is an equally important partner in this process and that is the business owner – your (potential) client.

As much as you need to be ready to play this bigger role with your clients, they need to be equally ready in their business to hire an OBM.

How do you know if a client is ready to hire an OBM?

There are many business owners who are eager to hire an OBM, but not all of them are ready to do so, even if they think they are. Here are a few key things to look for when talking to a potential new client or considering whether your current clients are ready.

Clearly defined and proven business model

The role of the OBM is to help grow an existing business, so the business owner needs to have a firmly established and proven business model. They know who their target market is. They know exactly how they make their money – what are they selling, who is buying it and how all of their products and services fit together.

If they are a brand new business or are struggling, an OBM is a bad idea. An OBM is an accelerant or catalyst that can create great results, but needs a foundation to stand on. Asking a client who isn't already experiencing a modicum of success to take on an OBM can be like asking a kayak to go out into the wide open ocean – it's way too much too soon. The business owner needs to get their business established first before they bring on an OBM.

Steady revenue stream(s)

Hand-in-hand with having a proven business model is having a steady stream of revenue. In general, a business is ready to hire an OBM if they have at least a 6-figure income that is steady and reliable throughout the year. If they make less or if their income is not yet reliable (lots of peaks and valleys) this can be an indicator that they don't have a strong proven business model and they may not be ready yet to hire an OBM.

Passion, vision and goals

How passionate is the business owner about their business? Do they have a clear vision of what they want to achieve and a set path of how they are going to get there? This is the heart of any growing business and is NOT an area that can be delegated to an OBM.

Beware of the business owner who lacks enthusiasm and is just looking for someone to "take over" their business for them. It could be that they are burnt out, or perhaps just bored with their business. An OBM is there to help bring the business owners vision to life, not to create the vision for them.

Sidenote

I recently received a great question from a business owner:

Shouldn't [an OBM] be building their own business rather than building mine?

A good business manager doesn't necessarily want to build their own business. I like to look at business as the marriage of **vision (passion) + implementation**. A business manager is driven by implementation. We like to take an idea and bring it to life; we aren't necessarily the ones who like to come up with the ideas or vision ourselves.

Most business owners, on the other hand, are really strong on the ideas or vision side of things but need help with the implementation and management side. I joke with a client of mine that I'm too busy "getting stuff done" to try and come up with ideas of my own! And I like it that way, as I find it very fulfilling to help my clients bring their own ideas and vision to life.

Plus, if I am being paid on incentive then I am in a position to enjoy ongoing growth in my own income, similar to if it were my own business.

Likewise, a business owner could be passionate and excited about their business, but it may be something that isn't exciting to you at all. If you are working as a VA or other support professional, this scenario can be OK. However, if you are going to work as the client's OBM you absolutely NEED to be excited about what the client does. If it is boring to you, something you disagree with or if you have a moral issue with it, then trying to work with them at this level will be a real drag (and probably not successful in the long run).

Has worked successfully with a virtual team in the past

You want to work with a business owner who has experience successfully working with a virtually-based team, and in most cases they already have a team of contractors in place. Usually they will have worked with a VA (or two or more), a website designer, perhaps a copywriter, bookkeeper, etc. Any business that has created a strong foundation has usually done so with the efforts of more than just one person.

If a business owner has either a) never worked with a virtually-based team or b) has had really bad experiences working with a virtual team and hasn't been able to make it work, these are red flags. Before engaging with this client I would want to explore the reasons for this a bit further.

It could be that they have simply been doing it all on their own, and may need some guidance on how to start hiring and delegating. Or it could be that there are some serious control and/or delegation issues at play here that have made it impossible for the business owner to work effectively with anyone. As we already discussed, the "control freak" client is really hard to work with, especially at the OBM level.

They are ready to let go and share

The business owner truly needs to be in a place where they are ready to let go of some things in order to allow their business to grow. Without an OBM in place your client is most likely the one who is managing their current team members and plugged into their day-to-day activities. For most, it is a bit of a journey to let go of these day-to-day things and trust that their OBM will take care of it for them.

You also want to ensure that they are open to the option of incentive-based pay, which is really about sharing the wealth. Some business owners think this is great and really love the idea of having someone invested in their business at this level. Others may be totally new to the idea, and take a bit of time to warm up to the idea. Then there are business owners who say, "No way!" right off the bat, in which case they are not suitable OBM clients. If a business owner isn't willing to share in the results that you will help them create, then they are not yet ready to let go in order to take their business to the next level. They are still looking at their business as theirs only and won't be able to properly engage with an OBM.

They get what their job is as the business owner

This is probably one of the most important areas to explore with a potential client. What is their job as the business owner versus your job as the OBM? What expectations do they have of you as an OBM, and are those reasonable and achievable (as outlined in our previous chapters)? The business owner needs to stay plugged into a few key areas of their business, such as marketing (bringing in new business), development (new products and services) and leadership (providing the vision and heart of the business). Most anything outside of those areas can be delegated to the OBM.

Sidenote

Beware of the business owner who wants to give it all to their OBM!

You will come across some business owners who say they want to just "leave it all to my team so I can go sit on the beach somewhere." In my experience, this is a pipe dream more often than it is a reality. A business owner who wants to totally unplug themselves from their business needs to take a good long look at their situation. If they really don't want to be involved, maybe they need to sell the business instead of trying to hire someone to take it over for them. It's not fair or realistic for a business owner to just hand their business to someone and say, "Here you go, make me some money."

Online Business Manager Client Assessment and Intake Form

Here is a set of questions that we use when talking to potential OBM clients. The purpose is to ensure that the client is truly ready to hire an OBM and to see if there is compatibility for us to work together.

Feel free to use, tweak or add to this list as you see fit when talking to potential clients. I've added some notes for each question in *italics*. You can download your own copy of the Client Assessment and Intake Form from The OBM Toolbox at the end of this book.

1. **Tell me about your business. What is your vision? Why did you start your business?**

   How passionate is the person about their business? Do they have a big vision? Can you feel the "energy" of their business when they are talking? Or are they kinda blah or dull? You want to look for someone who is really "plugged in" to their business — you can hear in their voice how excited and passionate they are.

2. **Who is your target or niche market?**

   Does the person have a clearly defined niche market, or a group of people with similar challenges or interests that you can market to? Be aware if they are not clear on their niche market as they may need to do more work there before you start working with them.

3. **What is your current revenue level? How steady is your income?**

    You may or may not want to ask this question in the first conversation. If it seems to fit in the flow of the conversation, go for it. If not, then you can save this question for another conversation, but do make a point in asking it!

4. **What is your business model? What are you selling? What is your current 'path to money' or outline of your business funnel, with details at each level.**

    You want to come away with a really clear picture of exactly how they make their money – what are they selling, who is buying it and how do all of their products and services fit together. This ties into question 3 – do they have a proven business model that is providing a steady level of income, or are they still struggling a bit to make ends meet?

5. **What are your business goals for the next year? What do you want to accomplish?**

Have they given some thought to what they want to accomplish in the next year or in the next five years? This is super important – if they don't know yet what THEY want, you won't be able to help them get it. If they aren't clear on this yet they may need to hire a coach or business planning expert to help them create their goals. Also, are their goals achievable, e.g., creating four new products (feasible) versus overthrowing Donald Trump's business (probably not going to happen)?

6. **Who is currently on your team? What do they do for you?**

   It's important to know who is already on the team, including those who do ongoing work for them (e.g., VAs,) and also contractors (web designers, SEO experts, etc). Most clients have a number of people on their team and are looking for an OBM to help coordinate and manage all the pieces (which of course we do!).

7. **Where are the "gaps"' on your team? Are there any big challenges with your current team?**

   There must be gaps, otherwise why would they want to hire an OBM? You also want to know what any current challenges or issues are with their team so that you can come in ready to deal appropriately with a given situation.

8. **Why do you want to hire an OBM? What could an OBM do for you?**

    What are their expectations of an OBM? Do you think you could provide what they are looking for? Or does it sound like they are looking for another kind of professional (e.g., an SEO expert). Ensure that their expectations aren't out of line with what you know you are able to provide.

    Again, you want to keep an eye out for a business owner who just wants to abdicate their own role and turn everything over to the OBM.

9. **How willing are you to delegate? What is your experience with delegating and what kind of communication do you require to feel good about trusting your delegate?**

    This is SO important to clarify with a potential client. A huge part of working as an OBM with a new client is building the trust factor. You need to know what makes THEM feel they can trust a team member, and how or if they've been burned in the past.

Many business owners actually aren't that good at delegation, being that they start out as solo-preneurs doing everything themselves. So the chances are good that they may have some challenges with delegation and "letting go" of certain aspects of their business. It is the OBMs role to help them grow through this over time, as trust is built.

10. What questions do you have about the OBM role?

A good signal that a client is ready for an OBM are questions like:

- *What will the compensation be?*
- *Can we start out on one project first, to test our chemistry and work style?*

This is a great opportunity to really clarify the role of an OBM, particularly if the client is new to the idea of working with someone in this capacity. This is also a good time to talk about potential projects and clarify the difference between what you do as an OBM versus what a VA does.

Optional Questions, but still good to ask:

11. **How often does your current business encounter emergencies or last minute tasks?**

    Beware of a business owner who is constantly "'in crisis"!! This kind of chaotic and last-minute environment quite often comes from the personality of the business owner, and can be tough to work within or change.

    This can sometimes be hard to see during an initial conversation. Quite often you may not see chaos rear its ugly head until you jump in and do a project or two together.

12. **How much documentation or work process is already in place? Do you have a standard operating procedures guide or customer service policies?**

    If they do have documentation in place already, great! If not, this can be a great starting point or a first proj-ect to work on with a potential new client, since these pieces are essential for sustained growth.

13. **How much time off do you take in a year?**

    This can be telling as to what kind of work ethic and expectation they have. If they work 24/7, never see their kids, haven't been on vacation for years and are about to get divorced, this is something to explore. It could simply mean that they REALLY need to hire an OBM to help take the load off, or it could mean that they are addicted to their work and may expect the same from an OBM (yipes!).

CHAPTER

12

WHERE THE RUBBER MEETS THE ROAD

GETTING STARTED WITH YOU CLIENTS

Don't Get Married on the First Date

I like to say – somewhat tongue in cheek – that working as an OBM for your clients is much like a marriage. Both parties need to be committed to the business and each other in order for the partnership to work and the business to grow.

And so just like we do when considering a life partner, you want to "date" your potential OBM clients before you commit to working with each other. This is to ensure that there is compatibility in the working relationship, so that you can have a strong and long-lasting business relationship.

The first date

Let's say you've talked to a potential new client and have determined that they are ready for and could use the services of an OBM. Start with a "get to know you" project, something that doesn't require any serious long-term commitment but that will still be of value to the client (versus a "make work" kind of project).

The project itself could be anything. I like to ask the client, "What has been on your wish list for quite some time now that you haven't been able to complete or get to?" This could be anything from helping them launch that e-book that they wrote 6 months ago that has been sitting collecting dust to putting together a Standard Operating Procedures (SOP) guide. As I've mentioned earlier, helping to create an SOP can be a really great first date project, as it gives you the chance to get to know your client's business and see how things are being done (and how they can be improved!).

It doesn't really matter what you do for a first date project, what matters is that you get a real snapshot of what is going on in their business and what it is like to work together. Is communication smooth and enjoyable or are you struggling to connect with the client? Is the business owner willing to answer your questions or do they expect you to just figure it all out on your own? Is the business really making money or is the reality of their business a bit different than what they shared up front? Most importantly, are you having fun?

As they say in marriage, don't get married expecting that you will be able to fix the other person after the wedding. If you are struggling with the business owner in any way during the dating stage you need to seriously consider whether you want to commit to being their OBM. You should be able to tell after a few "dates" if this is someone that you would want to work with at the OBM level.

If everything goes great, you are excited by what the business is doing and you're having fun, then this could be a great OBM client. If you aren't having any fun and just aren't clicking with the business owner, then I highly recommend that you say no. Personality and communication styles are really important at this level, and it could be that there is simply someone else out there who is a better fit for their business (and more ideal clients out there for you as well!).

You need to earn it (and so do they)

The OBM role is something that is earned by both the OBM and the business owner.

This is what the dating process is really about – both parties getting to know each other and proving to each other who they are, what they stand for and what they are capable of. It is through the dating process that you earn the right to take on the OBM role. You are demonstrating that you have the attitude and skills that we talked about earlier (such as a marketing mindset and project management skills). Likewise, the client is proving to you that they themselves and their business are truly ready to take it up a notch with the support of an OBM.

I have people come to me all the time saying, "I need to hire an OBM to start today, where do I find one?"

My recommendation to them is that they don't hire someone off the street and pop them instantly into the OBM role. I have seen a number of business owners try to hire directly into the role and it simply does not work.

Why? Because they tried to get married first. Just like those crazy Vegas wedding stories that you hear about, if you get married before you even know each other, then chances are things will fall apart quickly.

What I recommend to business owners is that they let someone **earn the role**. It could be someone new who starts with a few dating projects (as already discussed) or it could be someone within their existing team who has the attitude, aptitude and desire to grow into this role (and I'll share more on that next).

Incentive-based pay is definitely something that MUST be earned. Although I am a huge fan of incentive-based pay, it is generally not something that you can include in the dating process. (You wouldn't open a joint bank account on the first date would you?)

Start first with hourly or project-based rates, and then when both you and your client have proven yourselves to each other and have made a commitment then **you earn the right to share in the wealth** of a growing business.

That being said, don't forget to let a potential client know upfront that as an OBM you will be asking for an incentive-based payment plan. After you've worked together and have identified a long-term fit, you can then discuss an incentive-based plan that will work for all concerned.

Transitioning to an OBM role with current clients

Your current clients may be ripe and ready for an OBM, and who better for the role than someone who already knows them and their business!

First, you want to make sure that they fit the readiness criteria in the previous chapter. It could be that some of your clients aren't quite there yet, in which case you just want to stay tuned for when they are ready. Be especially careful that you don't try to impose the OBM role on a business that isn't ready yet, even if you love the client and are really keen to help them grow their business. Prematurely taking on the role of OBM will put a lot of undue pressure on you and the business, and could make an existing client relationship fall apart.

The journey for a number of VAs who have transitioned is that they first take a look at their client list to decide a) who is ready and b) who they enjoy working with the most. This is a really good opportunity for you to let go of those that aren't your ideal clients and focus on working for a few that you enjoy the most.

The first step is to have a conversation with your clients about becoming their OBM. Let them know that you are making a change in your business to work with business owners at this level and that you would really love to explore this option with them since you enjoy working with them so much. Tell them about the role and how it is different from what you've been doing already. Let them know that you are excited to shift into the focus of growing their business versus just "doing stuff" in their business.

A few years ago Cindy had this conversation with one of her long time clients. "I scheduled a phone call with my client to let him know that I was making a change in my business. I shared how I was streamlining to work with just a few clients, and that I wanted him to be one of those clients. He was excited to have me shift into a more dedicated role. Being that we had already worked together for two years, he knew that I was committed to seeing his business grow. He also recognized that he couldn't do it all alone, and was quite happy to have someone help him out at this level."

After coming to agreement on her new role, Cindy took on more responsibility in her client's business. "I started managing all his websites, making sure content was up to date and coordinating with our web designers. I also took over managing event promotions and coordination. I now play a more visible role in the business, doing more marketing and making connections to represent the business. It's now been over two years since making this transition and his business has grown significantly."

You will also want to talk to them about shifting into an incentive-based payment plan. This is a new concept to most clients, so don't be surprised if they are a bit resistant to the idea at first. You may want to suggest that you give it a try with one project first and see how it goes.

Erin Blaskie of BSetc.ca shared a great example of how you can start being paid on incentive. One of her clients was launching a paid teleclass series and she

219

approached her with an offer. Being that her client would usually get about 30 people to join with her existing marketing methods, Erin proposed to her that if she helped her get more than 30 people to join the program, she would earn a percentage of the revenue. Her client was open to the idea and thrilled to have Erin so committed to her project. They ended up getting more than 60 people in the program which meant more money for both the business owner and for Erin.

If your client is excited about having you become their OBM, then away you go! Make sure to set up a new agreement that reflects your new responsibilities along with your new incentive package.

The actual transition itself can take some time, and is generally a matter of continually taking things off of your client's plate and also delegating to or hiring new team members to take all the "doing" off your plate as well.

13 IT'S ALL UP TO YOU

CREATING SUCCESS ON YOUR OWN TERMS

*"Faith is taking the first step even
when you don't see the whole staircase."*
• MARTIN LUTHER KING, JR.

What does success mean to you?

I find this to be such a fascinating question. When asked this question most people will at first say the usual things – making good money, finding a great relationship, having a nice house, going on vacation, etc. These are all worthy goals, but in and of themselves they generally don't bring the "feeling" of success along with them. How often do you hear of the person who has it all but is still miserable; it's an all too common story, it seems.

Success is much more about the feelings behind the "stuff" – what does it mean to you and your life to make good money? How will finding a great relationship add to your life? Why do you really want a nice house?

We've all heard the saying, "Be careful what you wish for, 'cause you just might get it!" It is REALLY important to take a look at what you want in life, and to truly understand **why you want it**. Otherwise you may get what you wish for, and realize that it doesn't matter to you or, in some cases, is actually a deterrent in your life.

For example, you could say "I want to make good money so that I don't have to worry about being able to pay my bills each month. I don't want to waste my energy on the negative and draining emotion of worry. I want to be able to focus that energy on having fun with my family instead."

Making money is the result, which really allows you to have more fun and light energy to share with your family. So the real success is not the money, it is the freedom of worry.

Once you are really clear on what it is you want and why, then **the next step is to ask for it.**

If you *ask* for specific results in your business (and life), chances are that you will achieve these results.

Let me share the story of how I **unintentionally** got started working as an Online Business Manager.

In the summer of 2002, my husband and I had sold our condo and were in the process of building a house. There was a period of time between when we had to move out of our condo and when we could move into our house, so we spent a few months living with some friends. During this time, we also had to somehow find another $5,000 for the remainder of the down payment on our new house, or else we would lose the house and essentially be homeless. On top of all of this, I had just quit my job to focus on my new coaching practice, which was not making much money yet.

I distinctly remember one night lying in bed and wondering how the heck we were going to get the extra $5,000 we needed for our new house. I REALLY didn't want to get a new job. There were no possibilities that I could think of, and so I simply put it out to the universe. I said, "All right, universe, here is the situation: We need to get an extra $5,000 in the next few months, and here's what I'm willing to do for that money." I wasn't sure what I was even looking for, but I did have a list of criteria which included working from home, having flexible hours and preferably in the coaching industry.

I kid you not, the very next day I received an email from

Andrea, who at the time was General Manager of Coach-Ville.com, a large coach membership and training organization. Her and I been in touch a few times on a couple of volunteer projects, and she was looking to hire someone part-time to work for CoachVille. The amount of hours and the rate worked out to be EXACTLY the amount of money that we needed for the rest of our down payment.

Let's just say I jumped on the opportunity, literally. And when I stopped jumping up and down for joy, I accepted the job and took this important first step in my virtual business. Not only did I get some great experience working for CoachVille (trial by fire, I like to say), I made some great connections that have continued to this day, most notably with Andrea.

The key point here is this – **I was VERY clear about what I wanted.** I was committed to being able to work from home. I knew exactly how much money I needed to make within a set time frame. And I really wanted to work in the industry that means the most to me – coaching.

And I wasn't afraid to ask for it, even though I honestly had no clue how or even if it would come about.

Although I didn't know it at the time, I was applying the principles of the Law of Attraction.

I consider the Law of Attraction to be the process of "let go and let God." Regardless of how you define God (higher power, universe, etc.), the Law of Attraction applies to everyone, and is a matter of getting clear on what you want, asking for it and being open to how it may show up in your life.

For some great resources on the Law of Attraction visit The OBM Toolbox at the back of the book.

Are you ready to play a bigger game?

I invite you to think big for your business and your life. Uncomfortably big, if you dare.

You may not know yet how to accomplish these big goals, but go ahead and ask, and let the Law of Attraction work for you.

To get you started on the process, take a few moments now and answer the following questions. If you aren't yet 100% sure on the answers, you may want to come back to this section at a later time. Maybe take a day off and go enjoy some time in nature – being relaxed can really help open up possibilities.

1. **How many hours a week do you want to work in your business?** Include all billable and non-billable time and be realistic. In a perfect world, we could all work two hours a week, but most of us will need to work at least 10 or more billable hours in a week to make any kind of decent income.

2. **Putting aside the notion of "time for money," how much revenue would you like to bring in with your business?** Again, be realistic but dare to dream here a bit. Don't settle for the amount you think you can make. Go ahead and ask for more, the "how" will come later.

3. **What are you willing to do to make this money? What are you NOT willing to do?** Be as specific as possible, based on your experience to date. For example, if you have a family, you may not be willing to travel. You also may not be able to make phone calls on behalf of your clients, if you're like me and you have a delightfully chatty 2 year old at home with you.

4. **How will having your dream business make you feel?** This may seem silly at first, but this is perhaps the most important question of all. Getting in touch with the feelings around your business is often the most crucial catalyst for making things happen. And if your goals don't inspire any strong feelings, then you need to revisit them.

Scratch the itch once and for all

I worked in a support role of some kind for the first five years after graduating from college. Two years as an Accounts Payable clerk, one year as an Executive Assistant, and then two years as a Marketing Coordinator.

All that time I always had the "'itch" – I wanted to do and be more than an assistant. Don't get me wrong, I absolutely respect and quite enjoy the role of the assistant. But for me it was a position that allowed me to hide behind whomever I was working for. I could play around a bit, do my work and not really have to stretch too much or take any risks. I worked for some great people and had some great experiences but the itch was always still there.

In 1999 I had the opportunity to go to work for a start-up web-based publications company. The owner Rob, who became a very good friend of mine, was a passionate and talented young man who was ready to go out and "grab life by the balls" (this was the tagline for the company). When he offered me a position with his start-up business I left my safe and cushy corporate job to take on the challenge. Scary, indeed, but I felt the calling and had to go for it.

That particular venture never did take off, however it introduced me to the world of working online (which was in its infancy back then) and started me on the path to where I am today.

229

BECOMING AN ONLINE BUSINESS MANAGER

My ultimate goal for this book is to scratch that itch for others out there who may be ready for more. From the VA who is about to burst to the professional who feels trapped in their corporate job, there is a really big world of opportunity for online based professionals. It may not be apparent to you yet, but if you have "the itch" then you have already started on the journey to more. I would be absolutely honoured if this book has provided you some inspiration and guidance for taking those steps.

I also encourage you to stay connected to others sharing this same journey. Find a network of like-minded professionals who you can brainstorm with and learn from (and even complain to, on those days when you need to vent). Look to forge relationships with people who will challenge you and lift you up – those who will call you out to play a bigger game than you would ever attempt on your own. We are creating such a group at OBMConnect.com, where you are certainly welcome to join us.

No great thing is accomplished alone, and I look forward to sharing this journey with you.